Gift to

Harold
Wiseman

OF DREAMS AND DEEDS

# of Dreams and Deeds

Dear Master, in whose life I see
All that I long and fail to be;
Let thy clear light forever shine.
To shame and guide this life of mine.

Though what I dream and what I do
In my poor days are always two,
Help me, oppressed by things undone,
O thou, whose dreams and deeds were one.

JOHN HUNTER

The Story of Optimist International

By

Gordon S. "Bish" Thompson

Published By Optimist International

Sincere thanks and grateful appreciation to Nicholas C. Mueller, Baltimore, Md., 1959-1960 President of Optimist International, who so very generously donated all typography for this book through his company, Modern Linotypers, Inc.

Preface

Frankly, I'm not sure what should go into this preface. I never wrote one before. For that matter, I never wrote a book before, either. But there are a few things I'd like to say and this seems the logical place to say them.

In 1964, I was appointed by President Carl L. Bowen, to the History of Optimism Committee, and I met several times with the chairman, C. Milton Morris of Denver, and the third member, Dr. Donald J. Twiss of Toronto. Together, we spent hours around the table at our International Office in St. Louis examining all available sources of information on early Optimism. Maurice F. Keathley, Jr., of Memphis, was a member of this committee for the two years, before I entered the picture.

The first issues of our Optimist magazine, minutes of board and executive committee meetings, transcripts of convention proceedings, all were studied page by page.

As we worked, my interest in the project intensified and my fascination with the material we assembled grew apace. It dawned on me that in learning more of the early, formative days of our organization I was developing a greater appreciation for what it really is and even more esteem for the men who had the vision, the character, the stature and the determination to lay so well its solid foundation stones.

In fact, my enthusiasm for the project, to which the committee had been assigned by 1962-63 Optimist International President John M. Grimland, Jr., increased to a point where one day, much to my own surprise, I heard myself volunteering to write the book myself!

In my own mind ours is a great story and I wanted to be the one to tell it.

More than two years went into preliminary research. About nine more months was required for final study and writing the manuscript. Not full time, of course, but I surprised myself again by how much time could be found to work on this sometimes frustrating and sometimes perplexing but always exciting task.

From all over the United States and Canada came help. Many hours of research and rounding up facts were spent on this book in my behalf by good Optimists. I wish it were possible to have included everything they contributed. They should be identified by name, at least, for theirs was fruitful work.

But it all could not go into the text, of course. Let each of them be assured now that the help they gave me, although they may not be able to pinpoint it in the finished product, was of vast importance. It enabled me to establish facts, double-check dates and, most important, to capture the true atmosphere that has surrounded Optimism since the day it was born.

The greatest reward, however, is mine alone. During this year of living hand-in-hand with Optimists of the past and the present, both here with us yet and those now dead, I have enriched my own Optimism a hundredfold. I have seen what Optimism can do to communities and to men. The inspiration received this past 12 months, I am sure, will remain with me all the days of my life.

There are, in all probability, some errors in our book. There are conclusions drawn that may not coincide with those you would draw. There are no doubt certain passages that do not agree with the way the story was told to you. For these transgressions I offer my apologies and assume full responsibility. I only hope the reader will take the trouble to point them out to me.

And, finally, let me express here my great appreciation to Milt and Don, and to Hugh H. Cranford who replaced me on the History of Optimism Committee; to the previous History of Optimism Committees; to many members of our staff, all of whom devoted so much of their time and skills to this effort; to several presidents of Optimist International and their Boards of Directors, who demonstrated their confidence in us to get the job done by letting us do it our own way; and to my "first wife" Terry, who, in addition to traveling and working with me without complaint, suffered with me in empathy the labor pains of giving birth to the book I hope you are about to read.

"Bish" Thompson

Evansville, Ind.

A NOTE ABOUT THE AUTHOR

Gordon S. "Bish" Thompson is a newspaper columnist and editorial writer for The Evansville (Ind.) Press, a Scripps-Howard newspaper. He also has had a daily radio program since 1947 and a weekly television program since 1964 in Evansville. He has traveled much of the nation as an after-dinner speaker and lecturer. He is a director of Franklin National Life Insurance Company of Fort Wayne, Ind.

Bish joined the Optimist Club of Evansville in 1950. He served his club as committee chairman and director until 1956 when he was an Honor Club president. He was a lieutenant governor of the Indiana District in 1957-58 along with 1965-66 Optimist International President John R. Olvey and, in 1959, followed him as governor. He served on the International Public Relations Committee in 1960-61 and was elected to the 1962-63 International Board of Directors. In 1965 he resigned from the History of Optimism Committee to write this book.

CHAPTER 1

T HE STORY OF OPTIMISM

began at least 500,000 years ago.

On that eventful morning Caveman Org called upon a neighbor. They had studied each other from a distance with both reserve and suspicion but they had never communicated. Each had gone about his simple and routine but vital duties without the other's aid.

"Good morning, Awrk," greeted Org in caveman language. "I have noticed that you have been having as lousy luck fishing as I have. Why don't we work together and push some of the boulders down into the stream? It would dam it up and make a pool. Then we could catch all the fish we can eat."

Awrk, with some misgivings for he'd never heard of such a thing, finally agreed. When they found one boulder too large for both of them working together they called upon Yuk, another caveman neighbor. He joined them in the labor and shared in the subsequent reward.

The above conversation and program, of course, required several tens of thousands of years to complete. Many lifetimes were devoted to the beginnings of the primitive instinct that men should join together for their common good, for protection, for comfort, for convenience and for progress.

As the generations and the centuries rolled by primitive associations—prompted by necessity—became the basic foundation for government. From them date our earliest religious, educational and professional organizations. Today no man can live without membership in one or more major groups—the state, the church, the family and the educational system, each must perpetuate itself if society is to continue.

In addition to these, in which we all hold membership, there are other associations. Many hundreds of thousands have come into being and later disappeared as the need for them died out. These are the voluntary unions of people who form some sort of formal organizational structure to bind them together simply because they share a particular occupation or common interest.

The common interests have been multitude and widely varied —from a fascination of Sherlock Holmes to an interest in raising gourds, from the urge to aid the natives of Borneo to the restoration of antique automobiles.

Even a simple listing of clubs, societies, lodges, association and fraternities that have come into being in the United States alone within the past one hundred years would fill dozens of books the size of this one. Even if compiled it would serve no other purpose than to be a literary curiosity.

From just a sampling of the thousands of such voluntary organizations, however, we may draw two rather important conclusions: First, such groups were rare on earth until the mid-1800s, second, they exist in significant number today only in those countries where freedom of thought, freedom of speech and freedom of action are enjoyed by the citizenry.

What was very likely the first Optimist club in the world did not operate under that banner at all. It was, actually, a "Non-Pessimist" club.

Sir Richard Steele: (1672-1729), co-founder and editor of The Tatler, was a member. There were in the organization, according to the Irish-born English playwright and dramatist, ten or 12 businessmen of similar inclinations and attitudes. Sir Richard, unfortunately, did not leave us a record of the purposes of the club but he did provide a clue as to its temperament. Any member who showed "Sourness of disposition," spoke impatiently to servants or exhibited any trace of pessimism was given the heave-ho forthwith. They called their group The Good Humor Club.

Although voluntary organizations were to play an increasingly important role in the development of society in both United States and Canada, they were almost non-existent during the early years of colonization. There were two reasons for this: The very business of providing the necessities of life in those hard years required just about all the strength and time the colonists had. Too, they were not free citizens in their own land and organizations of any kind among colonists were looked upon askance by the authorities of the several Mother Countries.

But as time passed and the once 13 colonies became a new nation, that almost from the outset gave evidence it would before long become one of the greatest powers for good under the sun, the gregarious instincts of the residents came to the surface.

Almost simultaneously across the land there sprang up all manner of voluntary organizations. While some of them were dedicated to trivial or unpopular causes, the great majority concerned themselves with the improvement of the world about them.

These organizations satisfied much more than their members' simple instinct for banding together for common good. They provided opportunity for the average or "little" man to have a hand in running things. Here he could gain a title, a responsibility and a measure of prestige. He could serve on a committee, participate in open forum and have audience for his two cents' worth. Here he could get in on community action and get a little recognition through his association with an organization designed for the public good.

The advent and growth of the service club parallels that of the industrial revolution in America. As the nation emerged from a predominately agricultural society—in which most men did most things for themselves—there also emerged a citizen whose horizons widened with each passing year and whose areas of interest and concern broadened accordingly.

Into the new era came social advances on every front. Women banded together to win a 50 year fight for the right to vote. Men and women joined forces to work for and secure the finest free public school education on earth for their children. In every city groups of voluntary organization members were discovering for themselves that when properly harnessed and energetically employed the forces they could generate were strong enough to change things.

And those who believed they could change things for the better called themselves "Optimists."

Just how many Optimist clubs there were in the United States and Canada before 1900 will never be known. There were several, however, for the name is listed among other organizations in rare old city directories and guides on library shelves. There is no evidence that any was aware another Optimist club existed anywhere.

One was in California. Its members were young men of the Methodist Episcopal church who selected "Optimist Club" to identify their group-within-a-group.

One of the earliest and certainly the most successful among these isolated Optimist clubs was organized in Cincinnati in 1895. In May of that year the constitution of "The Queen City Optimists Club" was adopted. Its members included men who figured prominently in the civic life of Cincinnati before the turn of the century. Its activities have down through the years been centered around efforts for the betterment of its home city, both in civic and cultural fields.

Although the Queen City Optimists Club has never affiliated itself with Optimist International, it has served its city effectively and continuously since its origin and its members still meet each Saturday noon at the Queen City Club in Cincinnati.

On November 11, 1905, the 129 members of "The Optimists Club" of Chicago held their "first annual banquet" at Vogelsang's in that city.

Again the evidence is meagre. All that is known today of that early day optimistic group is that it consisted of men both affluent and capable of enjoying the good things of life for theirs was a lavish banquet even by today's standards. Their six-course feast featured "Roast Filet of Beef Aux Champignons."

They also must have had an admirable capacity for oratory, too, for the program lists no less than 14 speakers. And that does not include the campaign "remarks" of six men who had announced themselves as "candidates for the directorate."

If this long-ago Chicago group celebrated its second annual banquet the following year, the event is lost to history.

No, there is no historic, documented chain of events that can be pointed to as forming the links between the earliest Optimist clubs and those which later moved toward unification and the founding of Optimist International.

It must be more than mere coincidence, however, that in many places within a period of a few years many men banded together under the same title and with fundamentally the same objectives. The reason should be apparent: Both the time and the men were ripe for Optimism.

And just what is this thing called Optimism?

There have been many definitions by many wise and articulate men. In its essence, though, Optimism is that inherent and unquenchable faith within a man that leaves no room for doubt about the future. Regardless of past conditions, current situations and future prospects, in the end Right will win out over Wrong. It is even more. True Optimism also demands an eager willingness to work hard and effectively toward the ultimate goal.

Perhaps Abraham Lincoln said it best: "Let us have faith that right makes might; and in that faith let us to the end dare to do our duty as we understand it."

There is no incident on record in which a man or a nation advanced, socially, culturally, politically, economically, morally or scientifically, without the vital ingredient of Optimism.

The philosophy of optimism transcends race, creed and economic station. It conflicts with no religion but enhances the value of all religions. It is at once simple to comprehend and difficult to define. With optimism a man, a community or a nation can accomplish that which seemed impossible. Without it the struggle is lost before it begins.

Because optimism has been a motivating factor among men since the beginning of time, it has always been true that optimists have sought out each other and then worked together for the common good and advancement of themselves and others about them.

"The history of Optimist International," Nicholas F. Nolan, an early international president, said, "follows the same pattern of any history: It is a long series of facing up to difficulties and overcoming them."

Oscar A. Smith, another early day president, added a second ingredient. "It was hard work, sure. But it was a lot of fun, too. In fact, the greatest single thing in Optimism is fellowship. It is good men getting together regularly. When they enjoy each other's company they work together in harmony. Friendships are built and much good is accomplished. Without fellowship no work would have been done: without work, the whole thing would never have gotten off the ground."

In the mind of Past International President Walter J. Pray, it's mostly a matter of leadership. "Good leadership makes good Optimist clubs that are worth something, that do something. Weak leadership leads but one way, for a service club or anything else . . . down!"

C. Edd Hall, still another past president of Optimist International, drew from his own experiences another basic premise. "Without a workable, constructive program all fellowship would be hollow, all work in vain and good leadership wasted. Optimist International has just such a constructive program. It offers a challenge to every member and provides a definite route over which the individual and the club may travel to the highest accomplishments."

In 1960 the late Leo F. Nohl, Milwaukee attorney and international president in 1925-1926, looked back over the early struggling years and drew about the same conclusions.

"In its inception," he wrote, "the clear motivation for the organization was that of good fellowship, taking its usual form of 'extra-curricular' parties, with little thought to propagandizing its adopted philosophy of Optimism.

"Then some local clubs ventured into the work of trying to redeem wayward male youths who had gotten into the juvenile courts. At first there was no definite plan or program, however, and those clubs that did attempt to befriend the boy engaged in such a wide variety of activities it did not serve a national purpose.

"In 1924 a group of seven delegates to the convention, on their own initiative, set up the beginnings of an international plan which, in the course of the years, has resulted in outstanding accomplishment. The great emotional appeal of helping boys on their way to manhood is increasing by the attraction to membership in Optimism."

From these and other men who were both witnesses of and participants in Optimism's early struggles we may find the answer as to why several independent "Optimist Clubs" flourished but briefly and then died while others grew on, gathering strength and prestige until such time as they began to band together to form the first framework for an international organization.

Fellowship . . . Constructive Program . . . Leadership. Upon these firm foundation stones has Optimist International been built.

CHAPTER 2

IT IS ONE OF THE MORE FASCINATING
quirks of history that the same man who made possible the gra-
cious and prosperous but almost feudal economic society of the
South, later was responsible for the revolutionary industrial system that was to blow it sky high during and after the Civil War.

His name was Eli Whitney. It was his cotton gin that paved
the path for the mass production of cotton with slave labor. It
was also Whitney's development of interchangeable parts for
firearms that enabled the Union to conquer the Confederacy in a
long and tragic conflict. After the war this same system of pro-
ducing identical parts for machinery instead of "custom building" each separate machine was applied to industry and the industrial revolution was on.

By the turn of the century mass production was beginning to
gather momentum. Ten years later it began to make its drastic
changes in world economics and social life. The automobile,
which until then had been a mechanical novelty, became part of

the business picture and instead of snorting and bucking along at an erratic and undependable five miles an hour was now chugging along at top speeds of 40 or 50 mph. Horizons were drawing closer and areas of business were widening. Men in business began to see farther than the next county.

E. L. Monser, a young insurance man of Buffalo, N. Y., was one of the pioneers in the idea of going out after business. On his return to Buffalo after a trip "in the West" early in 1911, he dropped around to the office of his friend, Charles Grein.

"Charlie," he said, "I've picked up what I think is a great idea. Why don't we organize a club of men from different businesses and professions and promote the old 'you scratch my back and I'll scratch yours' system? A man just naturally wants to do business with his friends and in such a club we would all be friends. I think it would be great for all of us."

There must have been more than a little enthusiasm and sincerity in the young insurance man's presentation, for Charles Grein was quick to buy the idea. He agreed to host a meeting in his office of Monser and three other men a few days later, on February 16.

With Monser and Grein on that day in 1911 were O. L. Neal, dealer in Victrolas and Indian motorcycles, Eugene Tanke, jeweler, and J. Raymond Schwartz, brewer.

"In these times," Monser told them, "it is mighty difficult for men in the business world to stand alone." And he outlined for them as he had for Grein, his idea of a club organized for mutual benefit.

"We'll call it The Optimist Club of Buffalo!"

Again his enthusiasm was infectious. For the next six weeks the five men devoted their attention, efforts and time to talking Optimist club possibilities to their friends in Buffalo business circles.

By April 1 they had interested 25 men in taking part in the organization of the club. On that date they met, agreed upon the fundamental purposes, time, place and regularity of meetings, and elected as their president John G. Schuler.

They were off to a flying start, these men of Buffalo, and

looked ahead to rapid progress in the building of their club and its rise to a high plateau of prestige in their city. But—

"There followed months of disappointment and delays," one of the founders was to write four year's later. It would take more than that, however, to dampen their enthusiasm or stall permanently their organizational machinery. As the writer added, "Since we had adopted the name of 'Optimist' nothing could come but success."

Even so, this early club continued to operate primarily for the benefit of its members.

"The club has become strong because it is modern," reported the historian of 1915. "The day of co-operation is at hand and an organization founded on principles of mutual benefit and co-operation is following the lines of true efficiency.

"Optimists help each other and in so doing they forge a chain of fraternal feeling which is unbreakable. The membership in the Optimist club is limited in the nature of things but this is a blessing not a misfortune, and since quantity is impossible, let quality be ever before us.

"Today the mother organization in Buffalo has two off-springs, one in Rochester and one in Syracuse. Optimism prevails everywhere! To become a national organization is merely to go on as we are in these three cities, as our momentum is not to be dented.

"All praise to those staunch Optimists who have remained from the beginning; never seeing anything but success and never admitting anything but progress."

These three clubs—Buffalo, Syracuse and Rochester—believed that it was most difficult for clubs, as well as men, to operate independently. Soon after the building of the Rochester club they incorporated as The Optimist Clubs of New York State. This was the first attempt toward any unification of Optimist clubs.

Members and officers of the clubs also soon learned another truth about service clubs, there is vastly more to be gained from helping others than from helping only themselves. The value of practicing the Golden Rule beyond the confines of membership is both greater and longer lasting than the mere monetary gains of business reciprocity.

First president of the Syracuse club was Sen. J. Henry Walters, at that time member of the New York state senate. It was under this urging and guidance that the Syracuse Optimists undertook what turned out to be the first in a long and impressive list of successful boys work programs. They began what they termed "Big Brother" work, with lads referred to them by the Probation Department of Syracuse.

The immensely satisfying emotional rewards of such a worthy activity was proved then and has been proved countless numbers of times since as thousands of Optimists have held out a helping hand to literally millions of boys groping their way to decent manhood and the good life.

That is what we call "the spirit of Optimism." It was a vital ingredient in the creation and the development of the earliest clubs. It is today the very essence of Optimist International. It is the driving force that has led Optimist clubs to even higher levels of service in their communities as they look beyond the needs of boys to find equally great needs in all age levels, in every stratum of life in their home towns and cities.

It is through service to others that man finds the complete satisfaction for his natural instinct for gregarious living.

There was one corner of the globe, however, where "the spirit of Optimism" was at something less than high tide. On June 28, 1914, a fatal pistol shot was fired at Sarajevo. It claimed but one life at the moment but it was to claim tens of thousands of others before its echoes had died away.

To happy, prosperous and ambitious men and women who read of it over their breakfast tables, the incident was of little more than casual interest. "Just another blow-up in the Balkans," they remarked to one another on their way to work. "They have them all the time over there. It won't amount to anything."

But it amounted to World War One.

For four years the war raged through Europe and still many gave it but passing attention and turned to other more pleasant and closer-to-home topics of the day. There were balloon ascensions, pie eating contests and the newest dance crazes like the Grizzly Bear, the Bunny Hop and the Turkey Trot. And even if Congress had brought in the nation's first income tax laws, they were only for those in the upper income echelons and would never affect the middle-class business man or the laborer or the poor man.

No, there was more pleasure in pursuing normal daily business opportunities and having lunch with friends downtown.

There were a handful of Indianapolis men who had been enjoying this noonhour custom. They gathered at the same table in their favorite restaurant to swap jokes and bits of business gossip, to discuss the day's news and to savor the satisfaction of fellowship that comes when good fellows get together.

On this particular day in March the weather was performing as it usually does that time of year. The grey, light drizzle of the morning had developed into a steady old-fashioned soaker by noon. One by one, the habitues of the large table by the big plate glass window came scampering in, dripping rainwater and showering the vicinity as they shook out hats, coats and umbrellas.

Their "entertainment" that day was hardly up to standard. They had been kidded often about their table at the window where they could indulge in girl-watching as they waited for their lunch to be served. Nor did they deny the allegation. But on that day there were few office girls and women shoppers on the walk and those whose duties did demand their exposure to the weather darted by too quickly to be given more than cursory examination through the rain streaked window.

One of the last to arrive that day was Edwin L. Quarles. He seemed surprised to find anyone else there.

"I thought I was the only optimist in the bunch," he said as he wiped the rain from his face with his handkerchief. "As I splashed my way over here I made a bet with myself I'd be the only one to show up. But I guess we're all just naturally confirmed optimists."

Then he had a sudden flash of inspiration.

"Maybe we ought to make a real club out of this bunch. Seems to me that what this world needs most on a day like this is an Optimist club."

21

FIFTEEN ORIGINAL MEMBERS OF THE OPTIMIST CLUB OF INDIANAPOLIS
Organized May, 1916

Top row, left to right: Charles Habig, James E. Trotter, W. T. McCullough, Frank E. Gates, Edwin Quarles, Dr. J. W. Ricketts, Joseph Raub.
Center row, left to right: Eli Schloss, Charles A. McKeand, Luman K. Babcock, R. L. Mellett, Sumner N. Clancy, A. W. McKeand.

That's one way the Old Timers of the Optimist Club of Indianapolis like to tell of their origin. Another authoritative source, however, insists it was Luman K. Babcock who first suggested the idea of an Optimist club for Indiana's capital city. And at the first convention of Optimist International another version was heard, that the idea was first broached by Quarles in the office of McKeand Service Company in Indianapolis. It is a matter of record that Charles A. McKeand and A. W. McKeand are listed in the club's roster of charter members along with Quarles and that Babcock was its first president.

In any event, there can be no doubt that what the world needed right then was optimism in large doses and that as soon as it was mentioned all those present were in instant accord. That would be the name of their club.

As the official history of the Optimist Club of Indianapolis puts it: "It is 1916 . . . Murad cigarettes are selling for 15¢ . . . railroad stocks are high . . . the expedition to capture Pancho Villa in Mexico is being led by a brigadier-general named Pershing . . . the war in Europe is in its second year . . . a headline in the Indianapolis Star states, 'United States at Brink of War with Germany is Belief of Officials in Washington' . . . hardly a time for optimism!"

A month after someone broached the suggestion of organizing the "lunch hour girl watchers" into an Optimist club about 15 business and professional men of Indianapolis sat down to a luncheon in the Claypool Hotel for the purpose of giving birth to what they thought would be the first Optimist club in the world.

None among them had ever heard of the Optimist Club of Buffalo or the other two clubs in the incorporated Optimist Clubs of New York State. So far as they knew, this was entirely original with them. Indeed, it was through publicity given the efforts to get the Indianapolis organization off the ground that the Indiana group and the New York clubs learned of each other's existence.

Not much was achieved, actually, at that first meeting on April 21st at the Claypool. Each man had his own ideas and though they agreed on the fundamentals they couldn't get down to brass tacks on how the first steps should be taken. They were in complete accord on one point, however. They should meet again and get organized. The time set was noon on May 5; the place, the English Hotel. Each man present was to try to bring two friends with him as guests.

Thirty-three men reported at the stipulated time and place. According to the club's history:

"This meeting was much more productive. Officers were appointed, plans were made and a constitution was drafted. Nothing was definitely approved but a substantial foundation was laid down. It was planned as a dual movement . . . a local club, and a national governing body . . . The American Optimists Clubs, with headquarters in Indianapolis."

Obviously, it was a bitter disappointment to the Optimists of Indianapolis when they learned theirs was not the first Optimist club in the world. They did—and still do—take understandable pride, however, in the fact that Optimism and what was to become Optimist International were visualized and brought into being on that day, May 5, 1916, in the English Hotel in Indianapolis.

It is also apparent that the "American Optimists Clubs with headquarters in Indianapolis" was a little more than the informal group had in mind when the idea to organize originated among them. The club's history makes mention that a "professional team of club organizers" was involved in the early days and it was probably at its insistence the scope of the organization was extended from the city limits of Indianapolis to the far boundaries of the United States as it was then constituted.

This theory is given further substance by the fact that before the year was out at least a half-dozen other Optimist clubs came into being from coast to coast.

In the words of Walter Pray, the team of professional organizers was responsible for "many of the chuckholes in the road that was ahead for Optimism." There was nothing wrong with the men who joined those early clubs, though. Make no mistake about that. They entered with enthusiasm for the precepts of Optimism and with clear vision of the possibilities that could be realized by adoption of and adherence to them.

Before the summer was over there were Optimist clubs (or

"Optimists clubs," as they first called themselves) in Washington, D. C.; St. Louis, Mo.; Louisville, Ky.; and Springfield, Ill. The Denver club followed in September and Milwaukee in October. The following year saw organization of the Optimist Club of Los Angeles in March, Kansas City, Mo., in August, St. Joseph, Mo., in October, and Kansas City, Kan., in December.

Acceptance of the new service clubs in these cities was so warm that within a year or two after their founding most of them consisted of between 100 and 200 members.

In May, 1917, the Indianapolis club celebrated its first birthday and issued invitations to all known clubs to send representatives to the first conference of "The American Optimists Clubs."

All these clubs, it must be presumed, were quite cognizant that they were member clubs of a national organization. The Milwaukee Journal of September 26, 1916, reported:

"A number of Milwaukeeans who choose to look at the brighter side of life formed a Milwaukee branch of the American Optimists (sic) Clubs in the Hotel Wisconsin Monday afternoon . . . A rally will be held on October 9th at which A. H. McKeand, national president, Indianapolis, will speak."

To that first conference at "national headquarters in Indianapolis" on May 18 and 19, 1917, came delegates from 13 clubs—Indianapolis, Louisville, St. Louis, Milwaukee, Denver, Chicago, Los Angeles, Washington, Peoria, Minneapolis, Springfield, Baltimore and St. Paul. (Dates for the first organizing of Optimist clubs in Chicago, Peoria, Minneapolis, Baltimore and St. Paul cannot now be definitely established.)

Although delegates to the conference came without authority to act in behalf of their club—for this was not a convention in any sense of the word—the sessions did generate a new feeling of unity within the national set-up and the men returned to their clubs filled for the first time with an awareness of the potential within their grasp. As it was reported: "Harmony was the keynote and every delegate seemed much impressed with the future of this new venture."

But time was against them. In that spring of 1917, the United States was making doughboys out of mechanics, school teachers and insurance salesmen. And Optimists, too. By the following

autumn all major industries had turned from peacetime production to manufacture of war material. Cost of living bounced upward 17 per cent, rationing of sugar and other commodities was
in effect. An influenza epidemic swept out of Camp Funston in
Kansas, bringing tragedy to thousands of homes across the entire
land.

These changes in the life of a people who merely wanted to go
on being happy and easy going had a troublesome effect on organizations as well as on families and businesses. Whatever upset
the economy of the nation, of course, also upset that of the individual and some of those individuals were the early-day professional organizers of The American Optimists Clubs who during
the prior two or three years had most likely been responsible for
the birth of the individual clubs.

Few were thinking optimistically that year and mighty few
were giving much serious thought to belonging to an Optimist
club. The financial obligations imposed upon the clubs by the
national organization and those required for the professional organizers became more and more difficult for the existing clubs to
meet. Newborn units, too, were something less than ecstatic over
them.

Here and there in Optimism were murmurings of discontent.
There was talk in several of the largest clubs of secession from
the American Optimists Clubs and the creation of a national
organization of their own.

Naturally, these clubs and their leaders looked to Indianapolis
as the "mother club"—or at least as the location of national
headquarters—for an indication of which way the wind was
blowing across Optimism. When the talk of secession reached a
dangerous point, the Indianapolis club took its first stand in the
controversy. Through its second president, William E. Smith
who was much better known as "Buttermilk," invitations were
sent to all clubs, disgruntled and satisfied, to come to Indianapolis for a second "conference."

In the entire history of Optimism there has been a no more
crucial meeting of club delegates than that held in Indianapolis
on March 21 and 22, 1919.

Eleven clubs were represented and that in itself is something of a major accomplishment. How could anyone persuade clubs to send representatives clear across the country to discuss peeves, air complaints and exchange bellyaches? This phenomenon, when examined closely in the light of that unhappy hour, is in itself a dramatic exhibition of the basic spirit and philosophy of Optimism.

Be that as it may, high commendation should go to the host club in Indianapolis for first assembling the delegates and then through friendly persuasion, tact and good humored diplomacy seeing to a successful conclusion a reorganization, and the amicable settlement of all major differences among the clubs.

Results of that two-day conference were both revolutionary and emphatic. First, they changed the name of their national organization from the American Optimist Clubs to International Optimist Club and incorporated the organization under that name, filing the papers with the Secretary of State of Indiana.

Next, a full complement of temporary officers and committees was selected and empowered to act until replaced by duly elected and appointed authorities.

Finally, and probably the most significant step, dates were set and a site named for the organization's first national convention. The seed of Optimist International was now in the ground and the first results could be expected on the 19th and 20th of June the same year, 1919, at the first convention in Louisville, Kentucky.

Delegates to the Indianapolis conference returned to their homes and clubs charged with new enthusiasm and completely imbued with the new spirit of Optimism. And all talk of secession ceased. Now the topic of conversation among Optimists, in club and board meetings and on the street was the event they were already calling the "First Annual Convention of the International Optimist Club."

CHAPTER 3

IT WAS A GREAT YEAR, 1919. World War I had been fought and won and now people believed there would never be another war. Everyone was filled with great hopes and bright expectations for the future. The boys had come back from "over there" and were again at work in the factories, turning out everything a happiness hungry public could ask for, from baseballs to baby buggies, from Ford cars to phonographs.

Great year for the young folks, too. A 17-year-old kid named Robert T. Jones came within a 9-iron shot of winning the United States Golf Association's amateur championship and all sports writers were convinced Bobby Jones would be heard from again because he "showed a lot of promise." Another youth climbed through the ropes of a boxing ring to score a TKO over Jess Willard and win the heavyweight championship of the world. His name was Jack Dempsey and the sporting world knew that barring accident, he'd reign for a long time to come.

Sir Barton won the Kentucky Derby in a breeze and before the year was out would become the first horse to win the Preakness and the Belmont to claim the Triple Crown.

Newspapers of the day were filled with wonderful happenings. Airmail service began between New York and Chicago. In the stockyards of the latter city hogs on the hoof brought the highest price known until that time, $2.50 per hundredweight. There had never been anything like these times in our history and there will never be again. It was a time of high hopes. And an ideal climate for the birth of Optimism on a national level.

From 11 cities came Optimists and their wives to line up 97 strong for the official photographer at the first convention of the International Optimist Club. When they assembled in the ballroom of the Tyler Hotel in Louisville to hear the welcoming address of the Honorable George Weissinger Smith, mayor of Louisville, they were in a rare mood. They were there to argue and then compromise, to demand and then yield, for all had come for the express purpose of laying the foundation stones of what would become a great organization and they knew it.

It is a remarkable fact that in the history of any good organization, governmental or private, the story is star-studded with incidents of the right man being in command at the right time. Such was certainly the case with Optimism and William Henry Harrison, first president of Optimist International.

Named for an ancestor, the ninth President of the United States, William Henry Harrison was described by those who knew him and observed him in action as presiding officer, without peer as a parliamentarian.

"In those early days when faction was arrayed against faction on the floor, Bill Harrison had the profound respect of everybody and his rulings were never appealed," is the way the late Frank O. Denney of Kansas City once described him.

He had been chosen president pro-tem at the Indianapolis conference and now was elected by the convention to the top administrative job for the coming year. Earl B. Bowman of St. Louis was elected first vice president; E. L. Monser of Buffalo, second vice president; Dr. Harry G. Hill, Indianapolis, secretary; and William C. Snyder of Kansas City, Mo., treasurer. Since the

Some of the nearly 100 who attended the June, 1919, convention of the International Optimist Club, now Optimist International. Third from left in center row is William H. Harrison, first International president; on extreme right in center row is Edgar Walsh, a member of the Optimist Club of St. Louis for more than 40 years.

heaviest share of the burden in new club building, in public relations and coordination of efforts by the individual clubs fell upon the shoulders of the secretary, it was logical to name Indianapolis as the headquarters city for the young organization.

First major piece of business for the convention was the drawing up of a new constitution, incorporating into it the purposes and precepts of the organization. For a starting place the delegates examined the constitution of the existing clubs. Here they made a remarkable discovery.

Although most of the clubs represented had sprung up in far-flung communities without much guidance from or even knowledge of each other and each had designed its own constitution and bylaws to suit itself, there was an almost phenomenal unanimity in their philosophy, their declarations of purpose and the mechanics of their club government. This striking similarity, indeed, was the key to unlock the doors to unification and nationalization.

There were two club constitutions that seemed to set forth best what it was the convention was after. One was that of the Indianapolis club, the other of the Chicago group. Each was examined, discussed and argued for in turn. In the end the delegates arrived, as they should have, at a compromise and drew from each proposed constitution its finest features. These, with various proper amendments, were forged into the first international constitution. Evidence as to how eminently well these men performed is found in how well their constitution served Optimism. It was not until the seventh convention in 1925 in Houston that additional amendments were considered necessary.

These 11 clubs were represented by delegates to the 1919 convention: Indianapolis, Louisville, St. Louis, Milwaukee, Denver, Kansas City, Mo., Kansas City, Kan., Syracuse, Buffalo, Chicago and St. Joseph, Mo.

On the inside cover of the convention booklet there is a list of Optimist clubs known by convention officials to be in existence at that time. They included the above clubs plus Los Angeles, Washington, D.C., Peoria, Springfield, Ill., Rochester and Cincinnati. During the convention there was mention of another club in Minneapolis. Other cities that had—or perhaps had had

—Optimist clubs at that time included San Diego, San Francisco, Baltimore, St. Paul and Grand Rapids. Several of these clubs and one or two of those represented at the convention dwindled and died within a few months and were not reorganized until several years had passed.

Dr. Hill of Indianapolis, International's first secretary, expressed the purpose and philosophy of its founders and set the pattern for Optimism as we have come to know it:

"Most men are optimists at heart. But we have never before organized their optimism. There has never been the banding together of men in our cities to create and spread the doctrine of hope, friendship, efficiency and progress. But since the beginning of Optimism it has spread like an irrepressible contagion.

"Our conception of an Optimist is a dreamer who does things. The ideal Optimist is a man of vision and a man of action. He is a dreamer, but he does not stop at being a dreamer, he brings things to pass. The three steps in the realization of a dream are (1) the realization that a thing can be done; (2) that he himself can do it; and (3) that he wills himself to do it. The third is probably the most important step of all."

In the year that followed the first convention, the original 11 clubs grew to 17 as new clubs were organized and most of the old ones came into the organization. By the time the second convention was called to order in St. Louis in 1920 Optimism as a way of life had taken root in the hearts of more than three thousand men.

Delegates to the second convention re-elected William Henry Harrison to the presidency. In addition to his exceptional qualifications as parliamentarian and administrator, there was a more practical thing going for him. He was the assistant superintendent of agencies for a large life insurance company and as part of his duties he traveled widely throughout the country as agency inspector. These trips on company business took him frequently to the widely scattered cities where there were Optimist clubs. These he found time to visit without expense to himself or the International Optimist Club, an organization that in those early, struggling years had a hard time finding money in its treasury for postage stamps and could find none at all for travel allowances for its chief executive.

As the months rolled by through 1921 and 1922 Optimism spread in all directions until by 1923 there were 59 clubs with 4500 members. This was something like the dream envisioned by its optimistic founders. And though the years ahead looked even more promising, there was one door that had not yet been opened, one avenue of progress that had not yet been entered.

From its birth at the Louisville convention the organization had been international by name only. Surely, somehow and someday, it could and would become international in fact. But how? And when?

During the holidays of that year, 1923, the answers came out of the blue in the form of a Christmas greeting telegram to the Optimist office from a young man in Toronto, Ontario.

And the door was opened.

CHAPTER 4

F ROM THIS DISTANCE
it is not difficult to see just how Optimist International grew
from a scattered handful of independent clubs to a well organized, co-ordinated and activated national organization in just
four years.

All the ingredients necessary for such growth and progress
were at hand and went into the program. Leadership, of course,
and communications and the enthusiastic efforts of many men
dedicated to the proposition that here was a philosophy and way
of life that meant something.

At the third annual convention in Springfield, Ill., the delegates elected to the presidency of the International Optimist
Club Cyrus Crane Willmore of St. Louis, a man of exceptional
talents and skills and the inner drive to employ them constantly
for the good of whatever it was that commanded his interest and
energies.

In the administrative year 1921-1922 Cy Willmore was interested in Optimism. He traveled over the United States at his own expense, strengthening and inspiring existing clubs with his infectious enthusiasm and creating new clubs in strange places almost single-handed by his persuasive, dynamic personality. He was a realtor and real estate developer and within the next few years was to make a million dollars and then see it wiped away in the Depression. Pausing only long enough to put on a clean shirt, he went back to work and made another million before he died. He towered as high in his field of work as he did in Optimism, and served well a term as president of the National Real Estate Boards.

At the end of his term as president of the International Optimist Club, Cy Willmore delivered a convention address that is still hailed by those who heard it as "probably the finest forensic effort in the history of our conventions." In his address he laid out the route for his dream of a great service organization "based on positive living and an affirmative philosophy." It could be accomplished. He had demonstrated that himself. During his term as president, he had brought new clubs into being at the phenomenal rate of almost two a month. Leadership? Early Optimism had it in massive supply when it was needed most.

From its inception, the lines of communication between clubs and individual members, were strengthened by the Optimist magazine. The first edition was published in October, 1920, from Indianapolis. Each of the 27 clubs then in existence was requested to appoint a "scribe" to report in at least once a month with news of his club, suggestions for the entire organization and optimistic thoughts about things in general.

On the front cover of some of those early issues appears a moon-shaped, smiling face. This beaming countenance had been suggested by a St. Louis Optimist as the official emblem of the International Optimist Club and it was so voted by the executive committee in August, 1922. Along with the smiling face there appeared another symbol. It had the sun in its center and the words "Friendship, Sociability, Loyalty, Reciprocity" around it as a border.

The moon-faced cheery chap and the four-word motto have

long since been replaced by more sophisticated and dignified symbols. At the time, however, the symbols were quite proper, for the '20s were not exactly sophisticated years.

Millions were fascinated by a new plaything called radio. One out of six people went to the movies each week to marvel at the acrobatics of Douglas Fairbanks, the winsome charms of Mary Pickford, the pantomime capers of Charlie Chaplin and the rugged heroism of that doughty cowboy, Tom Mix. It was an era of bathtub gin and bootleggers, shingle bobs and bellbottom pants, racoon coats and flagpole sitting contests . . . and the world was wheeling away on one grand and glorious fling.

Not all citizens, however, were devoted to acquiring and then blowing in easy money or in reckless, carefree pursuits of happiness. There were among them some men called Optimists who had been hard at work in and for their organization in the United States and now, suddenly and unexpectedly, saw a way to spread their philosophy and faith north of the United States-Canadian border.

Charles E. Ward, a charter member of the Optimist Club of Toronto, later expressed it like this: "The organization of the first Canadian club, to those of us who helped, was such an extraordinarily stimulating thing that for the rest of our lives we were influenced by it."

It all came about because a young man went looking for it, found it and did not rest until he had gotten it for himself and his friends in Toronto. His name was William M. Skilling and of course everybody called him "Bill." He had intended to become a minister but was graduated from the University of Toronto in 1915, just in time to join the Canadian Army and go overseas into the thick of World War One.

Never in his life had he been a robust fellow and the rigors of combat duty almost completely wrecked what health he had. After hospitalization in England he was returned to Canada and honorably discharged in 1920 as a war disability. Even his attempt to enter the ministry was ill-fated. His church could not ordain a man in such wretched health.

Bill Skilling had about hit bottom in the morale department when, while visiting in the States, he chanced to hear of a club of

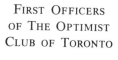

*William M. Skilling,
the man responsible for the formation
of the Optimist Club of Toronto.*

*Hussell A. Williams,
D.D.S.
Vice President*

*Cyril E. Dyson
Vice President*

*B. G. Stephenson, M.D.
President*

*William A. Hines
Vice President*

*Allan Griffin
Vice President*

men called "Optimists." The name intrigued him. Certainly if there was one thing he needed right now it was optimism. On his return home he wrote Optimist International.

Was there an Optimist club in Canada? No. Well, could he have authority to try to build one? Of course, and more power to you.

On December 21, 1923, Bill Skilling and two friends met to begin organization of the first Canadian Optimist club. Before they adjourned a telegram of Christmas greeting was sent to Optimist International and all Optimists everywhere. It was signed by Bill Skilling, Dr. Ben Stephenson and C. S. Dawes.

Those dedicated Optimists today who build new clubs with full support and abundant materials and expert guidance from Optimist International's huge supply of know-how can only look with unconcealed admiration at the new club building project of Bill Skilling and his "committee." The International Office in those early days could give them little more than encouragement as they worked and a round of applause when the job was done. And they were not yet Optimists themselves, officially.

Before long, however, they were holding regular meetings and more and more men were attending. These men, like those who invited them, knew little of the details of Optimism. But they did welcome the opportunity for wider business acquaintanceship, social fellowship, personal development, greater service to their community and all the other advantages of Optimism that quickly became apparent.

Yes, it was purely a bootstrap operation, a local effort stimulated by the zeal and enthusiasm of a young ex-soldier so wracked with physical disability he couldn't even get into the ministry. And as he was winning the battle for Optimism for Toronto, he also won his personal battle against ill health, disappointment, bitterness and, worst of all, pessimism and defeat.

The chartering of an Optimist club in Toronto was not only an incident of considerable importance to the city and for Canada, it was also an event of more than casual interest to Optimist International. Now it was in fact as well as in name truly an international organization.

This is why Toronto is understandably proud of the fact that it set the seal of international status upon Optimism, provided it with the prestige it so greatly desired and opened the way for the building of an even greater organization on both sides of the border. It is also why one frequently hears the Optimist Club of Toronto referred to as "the club that made Optimist International international."

On the night of February 26, 1924, at a banquet in the ballroom of the Prince George Hotel, the first Canadian club received its charter from the hand of James W. Chilton, president of Optimist International. Also present were the president and the secretary of the nearest club, Buffalo, N.Y., and the first Canadian field secretary. His name was William M. Skilling.

Bill Skilling had no intention of quitting now, just because the Toronto club was in business. Why, he was just getting warmed up. If he could not serve his fellow man in the pulpit he'd serve him at the luncheon table. What greater service could he perform than to spread Optimism through all of Canada?

And four months later, on June 4, 1924, the second Canadian Optimist club was chartered, in Hamilton, about 40 miles west of Toronto. Bill Skilling's dream of establishing clubs all over Canada, unfortunately, had to be shelved shortly thereafter. His spirit was willing, his belief in the worth of Optimism was unshaken and his faith in himself never wavered. But his long-suffering body was never really equal to the task. His already wretched health failed him entirely now and forced his retirement from the scene. He died in 1937, leaving behind a memorial he had built himself . . . the club that made Optimist International international.

CHAPTER 5

EIGHT OUT OF TEN SPEAKERS, when invited to address an Optimist club, feel obliged for some vague but apparently quite compelling reason to offer a new definition of an optimist. In the years since the founding of Optimism there have been hundreds of thousands of programs. And almost that many attempts to pinpoint just exactly what an optimist is.

These definitions range from the semi-serious ("The optimist keeps his eye on the doughnut; the pessimist, on the hole.") to the ridiculous ("An optimist is an 80-year-old man who gets married and then starts looking for a house near a school.")

All, of course, have been heard countless times by members of Optimist clubs who will; during the course of their memberships hear them again and again, patiently and politely and perhaps with indulgent chuckles in the appropriate places. For Optimists as a rule are amiable and agreeable audiences.

True optimism, however, is a far cry from the head-in-the-

sand attitude of the ostrich and the simpleminded Pollyanna philosophy that enables a bonny if unrealistic spirit to whistle a
happy tune while the world tumbles down around his ear. Real
optimism, as recognized by Optimists, is in its essence an uncomplicated faith that, though far from perfect, this is the best of all
worlds and that it is within the power of good men to make it
even better if they but will.

This conviction was not new with Optimism. It was not new
with Canada or America. Indeed, some of the earliest recorded
writings bear evidence that there have always been men who
through instinct or through mental process have been complete
optimists.

Once organized, Optimists began casting about for a motto, a
slogan or a creed they could live by. Many were suggested; none
were quite what was wanted and needed. Though each did contain the fundamental beliefs of Optimists, none seemed to offer
the entire philosophy in its entirety, concisely, crisply and completely.

In Los Angeles, Calif., soon after the end of World War One,
Mrs. James V. Westervelt clipped a little item from a newspaper
or magazine and saved it to show her husband. Jim was secretary-treasurer of the Optimist Club of Los Angeles, an office of
many duties including publishing the club bulletin and its yearbook, "The Desseminator."

"This struck me as a fine expression of what an Optimist
should try to do and be," she told her husband. "Perhaps you'd
like to use it."

Jim read it over and recognized it for its worth. He reprinted
it in the 1919 yearbook. He didn't know who the author was for
in the clipping it was identified merely as "Selected." The title
was simplicity itself: "Promise Yourself."

The little jewel of literary excellence and philosophical dyna-
mite contained ten resolutions, ten promises a man could make
to himself and which if they were kept, would guide him constantly and dependably along the upper trail.

Los Angeles Optimists, on finding "Promise Yourself" in their
club yearbook, seized it and took it for their own. Many copied
it from the book; more than a few memorized it. Two years later

when they journeyed north to recruit new Optimists and build new clubs in San Francisco and Oakland, they took it with them. In this pithy little document, they felt, could be found all that Optimism is and Optimists should be.

Among the Bay Area men to appreciate its value was the charter president of the Optimist Club of San Francisco, "Uncle" Bert Hubbard. One of his first official acts was to have it reprinted and copies distributed among all members of Optimist clubs in the vicinity . . . Like Jim Westervelt before him, Uncle Bert was unable to give credit to the author and again where the author's name usually appears it read, "Selected."

With so many California Optimists familiar with the choice and succinct bit of prose, it was inevitable that it find its way to the Optimist magazine and there it appeared—once more attributed to "Selected"—in the December, 1921, issue. Now all Optimists everywhere were exposed to it and were inspired by its simple truths.

When the next convention was called to order, in Kansas City, 1922, nearly every delegate present had a copy of "Promise Yourself" in his pocket. Hundreds of copies had been brought and distributed by Optimists of San Francisco and Oakland. Still without knowing the author, the convention adopted it as The Optimist Creed. Beginning with the August, 1922, convention issue the Creed became a regular feature of the Optimist magazine. No one knew who had written it but thousands knew it by heart, repeated it frequently and made it a rule of living optimistically yet realistically.

But Jim Westervelt was still curious. Who was the author of the Creed now officially the Optimists' own? He did a little literary detective work and it wasn't long before he had unveiled the mystery.

"Promise Yourself: appeared first in 1912 in a book titled "Your Forces and How to Use Them" and the author was Christian D. Larson. Its theme was simply "you can do anything you want to do if you only set your heart and mind to it." It was a small volume of high inspiration and philosophy, one of many like it which began appearing on the market shortly after the turn of the century and have enjoyed popularity and wide readership ever since. All were outgrowths of the philosophy of the "Transcendentalists" of the days of Ralph Waldo Emerson, Henry Thoreau, Amos Bronson Alcott, Nathaniel Hawthorne and Margaret Fuller. You wouldn't be far wrong if you called these people the first American Optimists for they discovered, explored and demonstrated the creative power of constructive thinking.

Christian D. Larson, who was to write 39 other books in addition to the one containing "Promise Yourself" and to give more than 5000 lectures, all soundly based on simple but bedrock precepts, began his career in Cincinnati, Ohio, in 1898. He lectured in public halls in the city, in homes of the suburbs and in surrounding towns. What he taught was received with active interest and enthusiasm and led to the founding of the New Thought Temple of Cincinnati. And this was to become one of the largest and most successful and influential institutions of its type.

Mr. Larson was also the founder of—and for 25 years the editor of and chief contributor to—a monthly publication called first "Eternal Progress" and later "New Progress." At one time its circulation reached 150,000 and there were subscribers in every English speaking country in the world. While on a lecture tour to the West Coast, Mr. Larson succumbed to the climatic charms of Southern California. In 1908 he moved his home and his publication to Los Angeles. Ten years later, while on a trip to Seattle, he met, wooed and married Miss Georgia DuBois, a concert violinist. To them were born two children.

The man who gave the Optimists their Creed continued to live in Los Angeles—a near-neighbor, incidentally, of the Westervelts who discovered it for them—until Mr. Larson's death in 1962. At each international convention until that time delegates telegraphed greetings and reaffirmed their appreciation of their Creed to its author.

The life and all the writing of Christian D. Larson provide today's Optimists with concrete evidence of the true value of the philosophy under which they live. From every one of his many books come lines to live by, little gems of practical wisdom that inspired so many when they first appeared and continue to inspire today.

Consider these thoughts, expressed by Mr. Larson even before he wrote The Optimist Creed:

"The Optimist lives under a clear sky; the pessimist lives in a fog.

"The pessimist hesitates, and loses both time and opportunity; the optimist makes the best use of everything now.

"The pessimist curbs his energies and concentrates his whole attention upon failure; the optimist gives all his thought and power to the attainment of success and arouses his faculties and forces to the highest point of efficiency.

"The pessimist pours cold water on the fires of his own ability; the optimist adds fuel to those fires.

"The optimist is a building force; the pessimist is always an obstacle in the way of progress."

As a matter of fact, The Optimist Creed in its original form contained 12 resolutions instead of the ten included in the Creed today. The two additional ones read:

"(Promise yourself—) To think well of yourself and to proclaim this fact to the world, not in loud words but in great deeds.

"To live in the faith that the whole world is on your side so long as you are true to the best that is in you."

In the countless times the original writing was copied by newspapers and periodicals—usually without the author's consent nor even his knowledge—both the name of the author and the last two resolutions were lost in the shuffle.

There is no accounting for the number of copies of their Creed printed and distributed by Optimist International, by Optimist clubs and by Optimists as individuals but certainly it must be up in the millions. Their Creed is not to be used only by and for themselves. It is to be shared with all others and has been distributed throughout the Free World for the benefit of all. Of course, it is in every Optimist's billfold for it is reprinted on the reverse side of his membership card. It may be seen on office desks, on the walls of homes, everywhere it may catch the eye and speak its philosophy of optimistic living. It has been distributed among young people, given out on the streets, sent in great number to remote corners of the globe where people are in need of a creed they can hold onto and live by.

It would be pure folly to say that every Optimist lives up to his Creed for that would demand perfection and no man is perfect. Likewise, it would be equally foolish to assert that men who are not Optimists cannot attain a high level of living because they do not have the Creed to guide them. It may be said with conviction, however, that every man, Optimist and non-Optimist alike, who has read, considered, remembered and made serious effort to follow The Optimist Creed is a better man for it.

It is here, in his Creed, that he finds the way and the inspiration for greater things, not for his international organization, not for his district and not his Optimist club but for the man himself. And throughout the United States and Canada there are thousands of men who sometime during each day pause for a moment to reaffirm the resolutions to himself he first made the day he joined an Optimist club and said along with the others:

THE OPTIMIST CREED

Promise Yourself—

To be so strong that nothing can disturb your peace of mind.

To talk health, happiness and prosperity to every person you meet.

To make all your friends feel that there is something in them.

To look at the sunny side of everything and make your optimism come true.

To think only of the best, to work only for the best and to expect only the best.

To be just as enthusiastic about the success of others as you are about your own.

To forget the mistakes of the past and press on to the greater achievements of the future.

To wear a cheerful countenance at all times and give every living creature you meet a smile.

To give so much time to the improvement of yourself that you have no time to criticize others.

To be too large for worry, too noble for anger, too strong for fear, and too happy to permit the presence of trouble.

CHAPTER 6

J OE SMITH, OPTIMIST,
is waiting for his plane in an airport half-a-continent from his
home town. A stranger drops his briefcase and sinks into the seat
beside him. His eyes fall on the octagonal pin in Joe's lapel. He
smiles warmly and now says one of two things.

He'll say, "An Optimist, I see. Say, you fellows have the greatest creed of any outfit I ever heard of. I'm not an Optimist but I
have your creed on the desk at my office . . ."

Or he'll say: "Optimist? So you're a friend of the boy!"

There can be little doubt about it. If there is any one thing for
which Optimism is known throughout the United States and
Canada other than its famous creed, it is its equally famous
motto: Friend of the Boy.

Since its inception, Optimism has been identified with and
commended for its program of effective and worthwhile work
with boys. All kinds of boys from every station in life are
brought into the atmosphere of and under the influence of Opti-

mism. They have but one thing in common, these millions of lads. Each one of them to a greater or lesser degree is intent upon becoming an adult citizen of note. It is the Optimist who, through any one of a great number of personal and club projects, devotes his time, energy, money and talents to assist the young chap in his efforts to grow into a man of decency and dignity as well as stature.

This idea of a man helping a boy is as old as civilization. The idea of an organized group of men pooling their efforts and thus helping many times more boys came later.

Earliest records indicate the first Optimist clubs soon became interested in the boys of their communities and took definite steps to help them. They show that it was not long after men began assembling as Optimists before the altruism of this basic philosophy led them away from their interest in helping each other through business reciprocity and into the desire to help someone else.

By the time of the first convention in Louisville in 1919, nearly every club was reporting some activity in the field of boys work. There was talk then of encouraging all clubs to do likewise, but no concrete program or procedure or even a slogan was suggested to the delegates. It is apparent that those gentlemen were too deeply engrossed in the vital business of gathering the several farflung and independent clubs into a national organization to devote themselves to launching its first major program.

But the Optimists, both as men and as clubs, were intensely interested already. Some were involved in the then popular Big Brother movement, an association designed to work with juvenile delinquents and lads who for one reason or another had already started on the downward trail. Because of this work by many Optimists, it was quite natural that some began to think of themselves as "Friend of the Delinquent Boy."

In many towns and cities men of prominence and influence were speaking up on the subject of juvenile problems. At the Kansas City Convention of the International Optimist Club in 1922, it was the subject of a major address by Dr. Charles W.

Hartloff, charter president of the new Optimist club in Evansville, Indiana.

A medical examiner in the Evansville school system and a past president of the Big Brother movement, Dr. Hartloff urged that "our Optimist organization accept the responsibility of helping the boy to help himself, not by imposing charity upon him, but by being a big brother to the boy, by setting an example for him, by giving him the right kind of advice, by seeing that he goes to Sunday School and by helping him secure the right kind of employment."

It was the doctor's theory that the greatest service an Optimist could perform for a boy was to convince him that Optimists are sincere in their efforts to help boys help themselves. This, he felt, would build up the lad's self-respect which in turn would strengthen his self-reliance and his determination to become a good man.

Response to the challenge delivered by Dr. Hartloff was both spontaneous and enthusiastic. Optimists everywhere were captivated by his suggestion they become officially, "Friend of the Delinquent Boy."

In the months that followed, word came from every direction that clubs were doing more than merely talking about the problem over their luncheon coffee.

Detroit: Forty boys taken off streets and sent to camp for ten days.

St. Louis: Many hours spent working with boys of Bellefontaine Farm.

Seattle: A camp for boys established in a park provided by the city.

Cleveland and Pittsburgh: Optimists work individually with boys referred to them by the juvenile judge.

Springfield, Ohio: Seventeen boys "adopted" from juvenile court and provided with memberships in the YMCA.

Milwaukee: Signed pledges from 50 Optimists that they would devote a specified number of hours each week in boys work.

Washington, D. C.: Supervision for the games room of the Boys Club financed by Optimists.

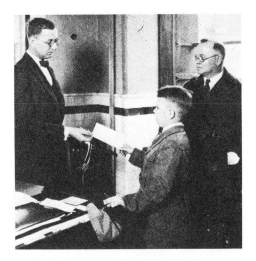

During Father and Son Week, sponsored by the Optimist Club of Omaha in 1924, John, nine-year-old son of Optimist Dr. O. F. Peebler, was appointed for one day state manager for a life insurance company. During his "day," John secured 26 applications for insurance and turned the proceeds over to the club which placed the money in the Optimist Club Poor Boys' Christmas Fund.

In the early 1920's the Optimist Club of Seattle erected and supported a lodge in Carkeek Park, a week-end camp for boys, which annually had over 1,200 boys enjoy its facilities.

Cincinnati: Fifty-three students helped through the university there through the Optimist Student Loan Fund.

Omaha: Wolf Packs organized in the lower districts for lads eight to 12 years old.

And from other cities, reports of other good work with and for boys.

By the time of the fifth convention in Chattanooga in 1923, when the organization's name was changed to Optimist International, the business of boys work was an item of prime importance on the slate of nearly every Optimist club in the land. Another keynote address, this one by M. P. Messer of Birmingham, inspired even more action.

"Optimist International," he declared, "must adopt as one of its objectives 'Help the delinquent boy and girl'."

It was Mr. Messer's contention—and he backed it up with statistics—that three-fourths of the world's misfits were those who had been improperly trained, that the child's educators had failed to prepare him for the vocation or profession for which he was most naturally inclined.

"Every large educational institution," he said, "should have a chair of scientific observation to study the character of each child and also to apply scientific tests as an aid in placing the child on his way to success."

This is good for Optimists to know, that as early as 1923 their organization was pioneering in a field that has become general practice today. The methods of vocational guidance proposed at the Chattanooga convention have since become common practice in nearly every public, parochial and private high school.

It was Jay C. Goodrich, then International Field Secretary, who told the convention: "We shall strive to make the Optimist club known to the world as the 'Friend of the Delinquent Boy'."

And Optimism's first slogan was officially adopted. It appeared on the front cover of the July, 1923, Optimist magazine for the first time.

It had become apparent at the Chattanooga convention that the problem of juvenile delinquency was a major one and common to all communities. It also appeared that here was a golden opportunity for both individual Optimists and Optimist clubs to

One of the first youth activities sponsored by the Optimist Club of Toronto was this harmonica band of the Jarvis Street Auxiliary School. The principal of the school was William J. Tamblyn, center rear, who became president of Optimist International in 1937-38.

Less fortunate children of San Francisco were annually treated to an all-day picnic by the Optimist Club San Francisco. H. A. Binder, club president in 1922-23, chats with several of the youngsters.

engage in a worthy activity that could easily become Optimism's first project. In the months that followed, much time in both national and local committee meetings was devoted to the study and discussion of how the problem might best be met.

From Milwaukee, selected as host city to the 1924 convention, came the broad and not too subtle hint that when the delegates assembled there they should come prepared to hear and talk more about boys work than they ever had before. The proposition was not met with disfavor.

In preparing for the convention, Milwaukee wrote to the International Office to ask if there had been created a definite program that local clubs could follow in carrying out the work with young delinquents.

It was a query that today is answered promptly and emphatically and followed up with step-by-step details of not one but many workable and effective programs. But not in 1924. The still young and inexperienced Optimist International could only reply that it had no definite plan to recommend, that the only advice it could give was to "tackle the problem along general lines," and the suggestion that local Optimist clubs co-operate with the Big Brother movement and other organizations already set up for the purpose.

Well, don't worry about it, said Milwaukee. When convention time comes 'round, we'll have it all worked out.

And during the sessions the results of their labors were presented in the form of a resolution.

In the first place, they disapproved of the word "delinquent" in the Optimist slogan. That was poor psychology. And while much of the work was actually being done among lads with records in juvenile court there were still many hundreds of other boys brought into the program who by any stretch of the imagination could not be classed as delinquent. They proposed that the word be dropped from the slogan and that the national committee involved in boys work be known as the "Big Brother Committee" or perhaps even the "Help the Boy Committee."

The Milwaukee resolution, therefore, included the following:

"That the program of Optimists be extended in the form of a

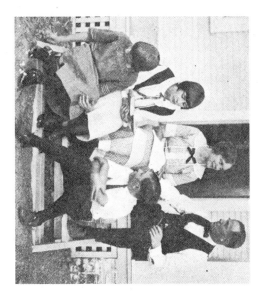

In 1925 the Bright Side movement, developed by the Optimist Club of Denver, provided modern, four-room cottages for indigent families. This series of pictures shows the development of the first of several cottages, which were offered to such families at a low rental figure.

big brother movement and that no boy helped by an Optimist club be stamped as delinquent, even by inference, and—

"That a pledge be secured by Optimist clubs from their members: 'I cheerfully pledge myself to devote not less than — hours per week to one or more boys during the year following the signing of this pledge. I promise to cooperate with the Boys Work Committee of this club and to report on this pledge on call of the president of this club'."

This was a good place to start. If there was going to be any major push toward getting all of Optimism on the Boys Work Road, the first steps would have to be taken by the individual members. Soliciting of personal pledges from Optimists by their own club officers began soon after their return from the convention.

Optimist International began making good its promise to boys. It mattered not how each club approached the work, whether it would be a helping hand to boys found on the street, to those referred by the courts, to those pointed oùt by social agencies or schools. Nor did it make any difference how the helping hand was extended, as an individual boost or through clubs, teams or other groups.

Main thing now was for each club to find boys who needed a friend and then give him that friendship in any way practical.

The August, 1924, Optimist magazine carried a copy of the resolution pertaining to boys work and also the individual member's pledge. The issue of the month before had carried the new official slogan, "Friend of the Boy."

A standing committee was appointed to carry on the work of organizing the great power of Optimism and channeling it along the most effective lines. The committee was charged with the publishing of regular reports on its results.

In obeyance of a convention resolution, the executive committee began at once "to develop a plan for financing the salary of an expert in boys work who shall have charge of further developing and carrying on boys work by Optimist International."

The farther these pioneering Optimists got into the thing the more convinced they became that if this "Friend of the Boy" business was to get off the ground someone was going to have to direct it. It had to have some coordination and a drawing together of the independent stumblings and hit-or-miss methods then in use.

Questionnaires were prepared and mailed to all clubs, asking what kinds of boys work they were trying to do, how successful had they been and if they had any ideas for the international planning.

Some were returned with sketchy information. Others answered by saying they were pretty confused about the whole thing. Still others registered surprise. They didn't even know they were supposed to be doing boys work. Many clubs didn't respond at all.

When Optimists gathered in Houston for their seventh convention, the boys work picture was a dim one. With what little information he had collected, Boys Work Chairman Leo F. Nohl made his report.

In essence, he said it was a mess and what was needed right now was someone to yank it into shape, someone who knows his business. That man, he recommended, should be Bert Hall of Milwaukee.

Bert Hall's entire life was devoted to boys work. He had joined the Optimist Club of Milwaukee early in 1923 and was a natural to fill the job of boys work committee chairman. His work in that capacity was widely known throughout Optimism. He had proved that he was indeed the man now needed so desperately to organize all boys work for Optimist International.

All he had to do now was bring order out of chaos, to establish a systematic method of assembling vital information and of organizing that information into simple and orderly reports that could in turn be of great value to all clubs.

Bert Hall died in 1933 but as long as there is an Optimist club in existence, he will be pointed to as the man who laid the foundation for what has become one of the finest and most effective boys work programs in the world.

Under his guidance and later under those who followed him in office, Optimists have approached their work with boys in both humility and understanding. Their efforts have been not to establish new activities or programs for boys that might possibly compete with existing ones like Boy Scouts, Boys Clubs, YMCA and Little League, but to serve and assist these groups in any and every way they can.

It is true, as a consequence, that many fine services have been performed in communities by Optimists that have been neither publicized nor recorded. It really doesn't matter. Rewards for such service are rich indeed and are found in the hearts of those who perform them much more frequently than in newspapers or in record books.

CHAPTER 7

A FEW DAYS AFTER SCHOOL STARTED
in Milwaukee in 1920 a member of the Optimist club of that city
received a phone call from the YMCA secretary.

"Henry," he said, "we've got a project going here and we need
your help."

Henry Scarborough heard him out.

The "project" was a "Find Yourself" campaign for the boys of
Milwaukee, both 'Y' boys and non-members. The object was to
help the lads discover their aptitudes and make the right choice
of vocation for which they could prepare. Henry Scarborough
was well-known in his home city as experienced in both vocational guidance and personnel relations. He was also very much
a "friend of the boy" long before that slogan went up on Optimist banners across the land.

Now he was being asked to do a job that was right down his
alley. He accepted without hesitation.

For several week-ends Henry Scarborough served as interviewer and counselor in the "Find Yourself" campaign. And from those sessions came a permanent organization of boys who had found in this dedicated Optimist an understanding friend and a wise counselor. They wanted to remain together as a group and they wanted his Optimist club to stay with them.

Henry agreed to serve their boy-type club as sponsor. When a proper name for the club came up for discussion, the boys had a logical choice.

"Mr. Scarborough, you're a member of an Optimist club for men. Would it be OK if we called ours the Junior Optimist club?"

"I'm sure it will be OK," he said and was proud of their choice.

The original Junior Optimist club adopted a constitution, worked out its bylaws and objectives and began to meet regularly. When summer came again the young members were brought even closer together by picnics, parties and camping trips. Like their elders before them, however, they weren't long in coming to realize that the richest rewards from such an organization come from helping others as well as themselves. They went to work for poor families, they lent the 'Y' an energetic hand in its membership, finance and "For Other Boys" campaigns.

And four years later, in 1924, when Optimist International convened in Milwaukee, that first Junior Optimist club was the hit of the convention. The rapid growth of Junior Optimism, the enthusiasm with which the boys entered it and the character building values it held for them were so obvious the next step was taken without delay.

The delegates voted the right of Optimist International to charter Junior Optimist clubs everywhere. The only provision was that each junior club must be under the supervision of a senior club and under the direct leadership of a member of a senior club.

In addition, the convention placed a charge upon the sponsoring clubs. "It shall be the duty of the member club sponsoring a Junior Optimist club to foster said organization, encourage its members and inculcate within them a love for God and country,

Members of the Junior Optimist of St. Louis posed for this photograph after a "banquet" given for them in 1924. Third from right in front row is Thomas B. Elliott, executive secretary for Optimist International and leader of the group. Immediately behind Tom is another Tom—Thomas Schaedel—president of the junior club.

The Optimist Club of Milwaukee entertained its Junior Optimist club at an annual Christmas dinner in 1924.

a respect for righteous citizenship and a true regard for the principles upon which the organization is founded."

The idea spread like wildfire across Optimism. It did not exactly stagnate in the city of Milwaukee, either, for Junior Optimism grew there from that first club of a handful of boys to a peak of 42 clubs and several hundred members in the years immediately prior to World War Two. It is good to note, too, that Henry Scarborough lived to see the full bloom on the tiny seed of an idea he'd had back in 1920. He died on December 30, 1952, at 94 years of age.

Milwaukee, however, was not the only city in which Junior Optimism had begun to flourish even before the 1924 convention there and the decision to grant charters from Optimist International.

In 1922 in St. Louis, an Optimist named Tom Elliott who, incidentally, later became executive secretary of Optimist International, pioneered along a similar trail. He was familiar with the tough neighborhoods of St. Louis and the boys who lived there without much chance of growing up to be anything but bums, hoodlums or even criminals. Perhaps if he got a few of them together and helped them organize a small club of some kind . . .

There were only five who showed up at the appointed time and place for the first meeting but before long the group had grown into a club of 30 to 40 members.

When Tom Elliott proposed that they be thinking of a name for their club he found the matter had already been settled.

"We call it the Optimist club," they told him. This was flattering to Tom and his own club but it also might be a little confusing.

"How about tacking the word 'Junior' on the front of your club name so folks won't be getting us mixed up?"

Within six weeks after the Milwaukee convention, the St. Louis Junior Optimist Club had met the requirements and applied for its charter. It was the first to be received and the charter was granted on August 5, 1924. It was Charter No. 1.

Two other clubs applied for charters before the year was out and then, on January 10, 1925, came the application from the oldest Junior Optimist club of them all, the one Henry Scarborough had started in Milwaukee. For a few months the Milwaukee club operated under Charter No. 4 but at a meeting of the International Executive Committee this was changed. In recognition of its claim as the original Junior Optimist club its charter was re-issued as No. 1-A.

The work of organizing Junior Optimist clubs proved popular with both Optimists and their young friends. In many cities Optimists did not stop with one club but created several, each with a membership of about 50 boys between 15 and 19.

In at least one city, Windsor, Ontario, the Junior Optimist club idea arrived just in time to prevent real trouble. Boys of the east side of the city and those of the west side had generated quite a rivalry. It grew more and more intense until finally it reached the "gang" stage with both sides ready and eager to meet on neutral territory and "slug it out." Police were called to break up the action.

Another adult arrived on the scene about the same time. He was the boys work chairman of his Optimist club. He was well aware of the situation and determined to see it end without violence or police action. First thing he did was to visit the favorite haunts of both teenage groups and talk with the young ringleaders. Somewhat to his surprise he found them not at all reluctant to discuss the matter with him nor were they unwilling to accept some friendly adult guidance.

"There are other men beside myself who are deeply concerned over this young 'war'," he told them. "What would you say to sitting down with us to talk this out? I believe that if four from each side of your hassle and four good men get together we can come up with something better than a king-size fistfight."

The boys agreed and their representatives reported as directed. The eight met with the Optimist, who was also a member of the Windsor YMCA staff, and his friends who included more Optimists. One was a Board of Education counselor, another a school principal and the fourth a former vice president of Optimist International.

It was plain from the start that there was no really bad feeling between these groups of boys. They were not hoodlums nor young criminals. Indeed, they showed a genuine interest in avoiding all signs of being bad boys. They talked freely. They shook hands all around and gave their word there would be no more threats of gang-fighting. They demonstrated clearly that with proper adult guidance they could solve their own problems.

One of the Optimist educators pointed out to the others after the boys had gone that while the schools stood ready to cooperate to the fullest with any youth training program, they could not provide one on their own. It should start out in the community and have both sponsorship and direction from someone other than their own school teachers.

"Well," another suggested, "we're all Optimists, aren't we? Let's get something started!"

They did and their efforts for the young people of Windsor did not stop with a Junior Optimist club. They sponsored a boys choir, lacrosse teams, an annual birdhouse building contest, seasonal parties and outings, a playground area and an athletic field and then threw in a skating rink on top of that.

As in many other American and Canadian towns and cities, Junior Optimist clubs flourished and their achievements were both high and impressive. Had there been no other effort made in boys work, this facet alone would have made Optimism worthwhile. But Optimists were hard at work in so many other kinds of programs for their friend, the boy. In general, the problems of youth in one city were about like those in any other. But each community had its own solution, its own best way to find the answer.

Consequently, a Boys Work Council was established in 1927. It consisted of five members with the director of boys work as chairman. It was handed a stiff assignment: Incorporate the best features of various boys work proposals and establish some broad lines of policy by which Optimist clubs could cooperate with all institutions, domestic, religious, political, judicial, educational, scientific and sociological.

The Council came to the 1928 convention with a program to recommend: Optimist clubs should continue their efforts in the Optimist Uncle plan (by which an individual Optimist becomes advisor, helper and friend of a boy referred to him by the juvenile courts), and the Junior Optimist clubs. They would also increase their efforts in behalf of existing agencies by providing memberships for boys in the YMCA, Boy Scouts or other character-building organizations.

By this time Optimists were getting down to business in the matter of boys work. The program had expanded greatly in the past few years and now was the time to provide it with the finances it needed to grow better as well as bigger. The delegates to the convention instructed the board of directors of Optimist International to set aside 25 cents of every Optimist's dues and use that fund for boys work on the International level exclusively.

Bert Hall and his Boys Work Council came to Asheville, N. C., and the convention with another plan, too. It was an oratorical contest for Junior Optimists.

Contestants and sponsors had little time to prepare for that first competition, actually. First anyone heard of it was when they received the May issue of the Optimist magazine, little more than 30 days before the convention.

"An innovation of unprecedented interest," was what the Council called it. The announcement went on to say that the contest would be open to all Junior Optimists 16 and younger. Each could choose his own subject, so long as it pertained to Optimism and boys work, and was to prepare his own oration, which was limited to ten minutes.

All Optimist clubs wishing to have their Junior Optimist clubs represented were invited to file their intention with Bert Hall. All entries were to be given opportunity to address the International convention. The Council announced there would be three prizes and certificates for the winners but didn't know yet what the prizes would be.

Records of the convention do not indicate how many lads took the speaker's platform that June day of 1928 in Asheville. They do state, however, that the first oratorical contest winner was a 12-year-old lad from Milwaukee, Carlo Pupero. His prize: a book, "The Americanization of Edward Bok." Three runners-up, each of whom received a certificate, a loving cup and a book, were Ramson Parker of Nashville, James Cherry of Asheville and Elbert Parish of Oklahoma City.

Carlo had selected for his oration, "What Junior Optimism Means to Me."

He told the delegates he was proud of his state, his home city and his nation, but, he was even more proud to be a member of Junior Optimist Club No. 12 of Milwaukee.

"The club to which I belong," he said, "is composed exclusively of Italian boys living in a district which is known as Milwaukee's 'Little Italy.' The ward is surrounded by the local gas works, garbage plant, railroad yards, numerous warehouses and the commission row. Some call it the slum district. For years our only playgrounds were the streets or alleys of the neighborhood where we mingled with the pushcarts of banana peddlers and played with the goats which infested our district.

"Some of the bolder of us for diversion hitched rides on freight cars while we explored the nearby freight yards for fuel and provisions. That state of affairs has undergone a complete change since the inception of our Junior Optimist club."

It was Bert Hall's idea, the boy told them, that this gang of kids, many of them on probation to Juvenile Court and none of them candidates for National Honor Society at school, could be converted into a club that would be a credit and a benefit to their community as well as themselves if a director could be found.

In two years, the Italian boy said, the lads of his former gang had become a club, complete with constitution, bylaws, officers and meetings conducted under Roberts' Rules of Order. Their year-long program of contests in oratory and athletics was climaxed by a two-week camping trip. From the word "Optimist," the boys had worked out their own personal goals—

"O" was for Obedience
"P" was for Patriotism
"T" was for Thrift
"I" was for Ideals
"M" was for Manners
"I" was for Industry
"S" was for Sportsmanship
"T" was for Truth.

Carlo Purpero, first place winner in the first Junior Optimist Oratorical Contest held at the 10th annual convention in Asheville, N.C., in 1928. Below, some of the delegates and families photographed in front of the headquarters, Battery Park Hotel.

Carlo concluded his prize winning oration by thanking the Optimists for the change they had made in the lives of himself and his contemporaries and added, "We want to grow up so that in the years to come we may be a credit to our benefactors and make them realize they have done something for the benefit of American boyhood."

Delegates to the tenth annual convention declared the oratorical contest to be the finest, most inspiring item on the agenda. They insisted the Director of Boys Work set up rules for future contests. Foreseeing that the next year would bring far too many boy orators to be heard, they ordered contests set up within districts with the winner of each representing his district at the 11th annual convention in Tulsa, Oklahoma.

And what of the 12 year old boy who "wanted to grow up to be a credit to his benefactors?"

He had completed high school and was three years into a pre-law course at Milwaukee State Teachers College—where Optimist friends helped him get a job so he could work his way through school—when his mother died, forcing him to forego his plans to be a lawyer. Shortly afterwards, however, an elderly couple sold Carlo their little restaurant and he was off on a new career as restaurateur.

Today, Carlo—now known as Carl—Pupero, his wife and their seven children live in Pomona, Calif., where he has made a name for himself as a business man, and proprietor of a popular chain of drive-in restaurants.

"I've heard winning orations in recent Optimist contests," he says, "and, believe me, I was never in their class. But that contest in Asheville so long ago gave me one thing I have never lost, the one thing to which I can attribute what success I have had—confidence in myself!"

Purpose of the oratorical contest, since its inception has been to provide a valuable self-improvement activity for boys. How well this purpose has been fulfilled may be found only by looking behind the scenes each spring where literally thousands of American and Canadian boys (the contest is now open to all boys who meet the general rules for qualifications) compete in club, zone, district and finally at the International level.

Carl L. Bowen, 1964-65 president of Optimist International, congratulates the $1,000 scholarship winner of the 1965 Boys' Oratorical Contest, Roderick M. Crossland. The three runners-up were, from left: William D. Arnold, Graham M. Hicks and James C. Bays.

College scholarships are awarded the four finalists, not books; other awards are made on district and club levels earlier in the contest.

The experience of preparing a speech and then standing on his feet to deliver his message to a group of adults develops in a young boy new strength. Future benefits, both for the boy and for his community, have been demonstrated many times since the first contest in 1928.

As one young chap, "washed out" at the district level, expressed it:

"Someday I want to join an Optimist club and help do for other boys some of the wonderful things you have done for me.

"When I was asked to enter your contest, I wanted to say No. My speaking until then consisted of reports in school, and even that always scared me to death. But my mother believed I could do it and she really worked with me . . .

"The speeches themselves have enriched my life . . . As I studied mine I began to realize what Optimism really is; to be optimistic myself. It dawned on me that perhaps others did not know about this and I saw that I was not merely making a speech, I had been given the opportunity to tell others what Optimism really is and to challenge them into being optimistic.

"I am sorry I did not win the district contest for you but I feel that I have won even though I lost . . . and I shall always be grateful."

Each year new thousands have the same opportunity. They prepare and deliver orations on "Today's Need for Optimism," "A Salute to our Generation," "Freedom, Our Most Precious Heritage," "The Power of Optimism" and other topics geared to challenge young minds into concrete thinking on, and clear expression of life's most valuable assets.

What of the ultimate results? They can scarcely be imagined, let alone evaluated. It is known, however, that across the depth and breadth of the North American continent there are thousands upon thousands of citizens who have experienced the thrill and reaped the benefits of participation in an Optimist International Oratorical Contest.

CHAPTER 8

By THE TIME
of the 1929 convention in Tulsa, Okla., Optimism, as a philosophy of life, was graduated beyond the first, struggling, fumbling years. It was beyond the state of a few enthusiastic and industrious clubs functioning in a few far flung cities. The idea had spread across international borders. Optimism began now to experience the "growing pains" of an organization expanding over the land faster than its succeeding administrations could keep up with it.

Membership by now included more than 8000, belonging to 117 clubs throughout the United States and Canada. In Tulsa Optimist International merged with Canopus International, a struggling organization of fewer than a dozen clubs but with the same general purposes.

Delegates to the convention in June, at the bidding of retiring Optimist International President Harlington Wood, gave further consideration to the sponsor system for club extension work and also to a revision of international dues. Optimism was spreading but more money was needed in the international treasury to meet its obligations and to take up the slack caused by certain clubs that were having a tough time, too, and were falling behind in their dues.

It could not be considered unusual or abnormal that Optimist delegates should turn their thoughts to finances. Although money seemed unimportant in the late 1920s and even though those were days of free spending, get-rich-quick and easy-come-easy-go, there were those more serious minded citizens who saw and interpreted the cloud on the horizon. Such good times, mostly purchased on margin, could not last forever, they said.

And they were right. On October 29, 1929, the stock market opened normally enough but suddenly prices began going down and down. Panic spread. The market closed for three days as financiers fought desperately for a return to "normal." But when they reopened the bottom dropped out. The party was over. Thousands now faced financial ruin. Some found the only solution in self destruction. The Great Depression was on. And everybody knew it.

Hardly on its feet, Optimism now faced its greatest challenge. Never were its philosophies so sorely needed; never before had the opportunity to serve been so great. With each passing month the need for someone, some organization, to be indeed a "Friend of the Boy" became more and more acute.

Many Optimists themselves were caught up in the swirling tide and, unable to maintain their own incomes, were forced to withdraw from their Optimist clubs. Membership rosters across the land began to dwindle. The international program suffered in turn as revenues from dues diminished.

It was typical of Optimists, however, that even as their number decreased, their labors in behalf of youth increased. There were twice as many Junior Optimist clubs in 1931 as there had been in 1929. As unrest and revolution smouldered overseas—with Japan invading Manchuria, Hitler burning the Reichstag and Mussolini making his first grandstand play as a dictator—Optimists of the United States and Canada tightened their belts and dug in. They added to their Creed an unofficial

Some of the merchandise displayed by 95 members of the Optimist Club of Minneapolis at an Optimist Exposition in 1935. Such expositions were sponsored during the depression years by many Optimist clubs in response to a Reciprocity Plan suggestion, which was developed to stimulate business.

Prize winning float in the Service Club Division, sponsored by the Optimist Club of Louisville, in a 1933 N.R.A. parade.

P.S. befitting the times: "Let us drive out business pessimism with the spirit of confidence."

In 1933 in the United States came Franklin D. Roosevelt and the New Deal, bringing with them the ill-fated National Recovery Act, designed to lift the nation out of the Depression. Many Optimist clubs went on record as supporting the NRA. Others participated in street parades staged to bolster economic morale. Still others turned their attention to the more practical business of trying to find jobs for men for whom there were no jobs and to alleviate as best they could the sufferings of their families. And during the grim 30s the number of youths aided by Optimists tripled.

At a meeting of the Executive Committee of Optimist International, International President V. Ernest Field of Indianapolis reported an emergency within the organization, a crisis comparable to that of the United States government itself.

"Losses in numbers and in morale, due to the times," he said, "are so heavy that if continued can mean the end of Optimist International.

To counteract this, he proposed a plan of progress built on Fellowship, Reciprocity, Membership, Boys Work and New Clubs.

"Our objective," President Field declared, "must be a net gain of 1500 members in clubs and 150 new clubs!"

Most Optimists, on hearing this, were willing to go back to the old precept of reciprocity if it would gain new members and retain the old ones. They did so with some misgivings, however, for the old timers among them cautioned of a lesson once learned, that men who became Optimists primarily to get business from fellow club members, and who subsequently failed to get the business they had anticipated, soon resigned, let their membership lapse or at least become inactive.

Therefore at the 1935 convention in St. Louis—the 17th—Optimists agreed as a matter of policy that business reciprocity among members was normally the natural result from close contact and friendship among those who worked together for others, and that too much emphasis on it for purposes of gaining members or in new club building could be harmful.

Also brought to the surface here was the fear that an ambitious boys program might throw too great a responsibility on already financially embarrassed club members and that elaborate and expensive programs for boys were creating a burden beyond what could be called reasonable during a financial crisis.

Still, the current reports showed many clubs carrying on with their effective programs and some even stepping up their efforts and responsibilities.

It was here the earnest and dedicated Optimists learned a simple but profound lesson: Clubs carrying out the most effective programs for boys and doing the most good in their communities were not always the ones that spent the most money. In other words, the true spirit of Optimism's declared desire to be a "Friend of the Boy" was based, not on money, but on the individual time and effort of Optimists.

Still, the fact could not be overlooked nor denied. "Money makes the mare go" and Optimism had no choice but to look the axiom squarely in the eye.

Sixteen new Optimist clubs had been established in the year 1933-34. These clubs were built by professionals of high calibre and were comprised of men of stature in their communities. But the funds of Optimist International were running low. Several dedicated veterans, most of whom had been in on Optimism from the start, signed a note together for sufficient funds to operate the balance of the year.

Henry Schaffert of Washington, D.C., was International President during the year 1934-35 and knew well the gravity of the situation for Optimism. During the following year, when Walter J. Pray of Indianapolis was President, he devoted much time and thought to the problem. Shortly before the 18th annual convention in Fort Worth in 1936, he approached President Pray with a plan.

It wasn't original with him, he was quick to assert, because he had seen it work with the Army-Navy Club, several country clubs and other organizations in Washington where the pinch of the times was felt as keenly as elsewhere on the continent. But could he take it to Fort Worth and propose it to the Optimists?

Walter Pray listened carefully, thought it through and agreed.

In June, Past President Schaffert addressed the delegates to the convention:

"I propose a new classification of membership in Optimism . . . Life Membership. The Life Membership is unusual in that Optimist International will get some ready cash with which to work and will not have to pay it back.

"Several members have offered to lend money to International to put over an extension program but this would mean Optimism would assume an obligation which must be repaid.

"A Life Membership is not something we expect every member to take. We are only going to ask those members to take it who want it.

"The plan is to sell a Life Membership for $100 cash—or a down payment of one third and two payments each six months thereafter.

"The officers who will have the duty and privilege of administrating these monies so received are men of sufficient calibre, honesty and sincerity that they will guard that money even more so than if it were their own."

"I want to tell you that I stayed up nights until two or three o'clock in the morning, trying to figure out a way to build clubs without money. It is just impossible to get enough of the type of men whom we need to go out and build clubs, without some assurance they are going to be able to eat and sleep while they are on the road. We need money to give these men something to live on!"

It was a sound idea and the convention's acceptance of it marked a great milestone down the road of Optimism. It was also a simple, easily understood and workable plan: Those Optimists who wished to do so could, for $100, pay their International dues for the rest of their lives. The dues they paid thenceforth to their local clubs would be reduced to the extent of the International dues. Money paid for Life Memberships would be used exclusively for the building of new clubs.

No sooner had Past President Schaffert finished speaking than A. S. Hull of Austin, Tex., was on his feet.

"I will buy Life Membership number one," he called out.

A split second behind him was John F. Tyrell of Milwaukee. "I want Life Membership number one and I'll raise you $50 for it!"

Mr. Hull responded to this with, "I will step aside in favor of a great Optimist because I have been in Optimism only one year."

President Walter Pray thanked the comparative newcomer and accepted the switch. Life Membership number one went to Mr. Tyrell, number two to Mr. Hull.

President Pray started to say he'd take number three but Thomas O'Keefe of Detroit (to become International President three years later) beat him to the punch. Walter Hofmann of Vernon, Tex., spoke up for number four and the President, exercising his prerogative, rapped for order and suspended the bidding until he could get his own name in the pot. And the President's name was listed as number five.

Others stampeded to get the floor. Mr. Pray recognized them in turn and Life Memberships went in a steady stream to F. E. Werneke of Louisville; Earl G. Stanza of St. Louis; C. E. Brown of St. Petersburg; Theodore F. Peirce, Lee Rose and Clyde Triplett of Los Angeles; C. C. Fletcher and Ralph Rupley of Houston; David W. Onan of Minneapolis; Fremont J. Hoehn of East St. Louis, Mo.; Ralph Monger of Knoxville and so on down the line until 100 Life Memberships had been taken and $10,000 had been pledged to Optimist International for new club building.

Results of the new expansion program were not long in arriving. During the following month, July, 1936, the Optimist magazine reported that a new record had been set for chartering new clubs in one month . . . four, in Columbia, Mo., Norfolk, Va., Jacksonville, Fla., and Hutchinson, Kan. The same issue reported that David "Ab" Jenkins, famous automobile speed champion from the Salt Flats, had been inducted into the Optimist Club of Salt Lake City.

Total membership, the next issue reported, had risen from 5540 in September, 1934, to 7020 in July, 1936. There were now 105 Junior Optimist clubs with 3099 members and the new junior club in St. Joseph, Mo., had gotten off to a sensational start, thanks to its charter night speaker, a Hollywood star known to thousands of boys and a favorite Saturday matinee hero to most of them, a man named Tom Mix.

By now Optimism had passed the low point in its battle against the Depression. Russell F. Meyer, who had been secretary-treasurer of Optimist International since September 1, 1928, was able to report to the 1937 convention in Cincinnati—the 19th—that since the low-water mark in October, 1933, when the roster of Optimists had dropped to about 4575, the gain had been both healthy and consistent.

"Our net membership increase during the year just ended," he said, "has been greater than that enjoyed during any preceding 12-month period in the history of Optimist International."

The grim days, apparently, were behind them. Optimists, along with millions of others, had finally whipped the depressed economy and were walking once more on the upward trail.

At the turn of the decade membership in Optimist International had climbed to 11,129 or more than twice what it had been just six years earlier, in 1934. But while the job at hand was stimulating it was also demanding and few Optimists—indeed, few Americans—paused to heed the danger signals that loomed large across both the Atlantic and Pacific. Few had little time to consider Winston Churchill's warning of a coming war that we, too, would have to fight. Few placed much importance on Hitler's army moving into the Rhineland, Mussolini's storming through Ethiopia or Franco's marching on Madrid.

In the Philippines they had a new U.S. Army commander, General Douglas MacArthur, only recently retired as U.S. Chief of Staff, and the new commander had an aide, Dwight D. Eisenhower. Optimists were more flattered than concerned when President Franklin D. Roosevelt appointed their International President, Thomas F. O'Keefe of Detroit, to his committee on Relief for Finland.

But it was true. The world as men knew it in 1940 was beginning to crumble around the edges. Soon it would all but disappear in a holocaust of war that would spread around the globe and involve nearly every civilized nation. Optimism, a philosophy that had stood man in good stead during the Depression,

Henry Schaffert, 1934-35 president of Optimist International, second from left, presents the charter to Edward S. Ferebee, president of the newly-formed Optimist Club of Norfolk, Va., in June, 1936.

David "Ab" Jenkins, internationally renowned champion of speed and endurance, was inducted into membership of the Optimist Club of Salt Lake City in July, 1936.

Movie actor Tom Mix, idol of millions of youngsters in the 1930's, presented the charter in June, 1936, to the Junior Optimist club, sponsored by the Optimist Club of St. Joseph, Mo.

would now be called upon to provide greater strength, to make greater sacrifices and to carry man through darker hours than he had ever known.

That it survived World War Two at all, let alone emerge greater and stronger than ever, is evidence enough that the fundamental truths upon which it is based, the calibre of man it attracts and the effectiveness of the service it renders are not only needed but sought out by individuals of all ages and communities of all sizes in a weary, frustrated world.

CHAPTER 9

T HE SURPRISE ATTACK
on Pearl Harbor by the Japanese Air Force on December 7,
1941, destroyed more Navy vessels than the United States had
lost in all of World War One.

It also left in stunned dismay a nation of freedom loving
people who had seen the war clouds gathering over Europe but
had kept hoping in vain they could continue living as they had
been, easy going, happy and well on the way to an era of prosperity following the grim years of economic depression.

Now their dream had been shattered. They had no choice now
but to buckle down to the task of fighting and winning what they
knew at the outset would be a long and costly global war. Congress declared war on Japan and upon Germany and Italy.

Meanwhile, in Canada, World War Two was already a grim
and costly experience. On September 1, 1939, Nazi Germany
had defied the rest of the world, had scorned its treaties and had
marched into all but defenseless Poland. Two days later Great

Britain and France had declared war on Germany. One week later, on September 10, Canada had entered into the war and taken its first steps along the torturous trail now begun by the United States.

It was to be all-out war that was to leave no industry, no business or profession, no home or individual untouched. Both Canada and United States halted peacetime pursuits. From across the continent came the cream of young manhood to make up the greatest fighting force the world has ever seen.

In both nations, civilians turned full attention and devoted every effort to production of the materials of war. Daily those who toiled on the homefront reminded each other: "If it won't help win the war, forget it!"

There were those who at first believed that all service clubs should be disbanded for the duration. Of course, Optimist clubs in both the United States and Canada had been quick to pledge their support to their governments and to promise manpower necessary for all community wartime projects. But would pledges and promises help win the war?

The answer was not long in coming. Before many months of war production had passed it became apparent that normal peacetime supplies of scrap metal would soon be exhausted in the all-out manufacture of arms and munitions. United States called upon its citizens at home to salvage 17-million tons of scrap metal.

Optimist International rushed to all clubs full instructions on how to organize, publicize and conduct such a campaign in their respective communities.

Following the first great campaign it was learned that an average of 25 Optimists per club had worked to get in the scrap, the more than 250 clubs ramrodding local campaigns had produced an average per club of 12½ tons of vital material and that several communities had selected Optimists as community campaign chairmen.

Optimist International's concerted effort in this and many subsequent homefront campaigns during World War Two is considered by many as the organization's highest achievement.

In Canada, as elsewhere, there was growing concern for the

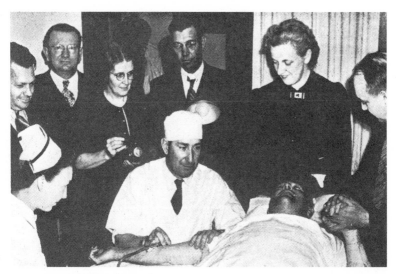

Members of the Optimist Club of Corpus Christi, Tex., donate blood to the blood plasma bank during the early years of World War II.

A "rubber tree" planted by the Optimist Club of Northside, St. Louis, in 1942, was this club's plan to push the rubber scrap drive so necessary to the war effort.

needs of children living overseas where the fighting was. Out of this concern there arose a project that was to spread across the nation and appeal to hundreds of thousands of Canadians. It was a simple and uncomplicated program originated within the Optimist Club of Welland, Ontario. It was based on the conviction that children were entitled to a few little luxuries just because they are children and that the war had deprived them of these as well as many of life's necessities. Should not the children of England have at least one taste of candy while they were growing up?

So the Chocolate Fund was created. With the Optimists leading the way Canadians contributed generously. By the war's end Canadian Optimists had packed and delivered to British children through the British Food Ministry, the schools and the Red Cross, more than 2-million bars of chocolate. For thousands of youngsters this was the only sweet they knew during ten years of war and candy famine.

The value of good service organizations, like Optimist International, to the war effort was proved in many other ways, too, time and again. Millions of dollars were raised in Optimist sponsored war bond drives. More than 1600 Life Memberships were purchased with $100 war bonds. Servicemen's centers at home were provided and staffed by Optimists. Untold thousands of servicemen overseas received letters and gifts from the Optimist clubs in their home towns.

Optimist International received a special citation from the War Production Board for its achievements in collecting thousands of tons of sorely needed scrap metal and rubber. And by the end of the war nearly 2000 Optimists were in their countries' uniforms, some of them to die there.

Along with every other organization, Optimist International found its program of growth and development severely restricted by the war. Its field staff resigned in 1942 to enter military service and new club building came to an abrupt standstill. Fewer than a dozen new clubs were chartered during the years of hostilities. It is interesting to note, however, that during this period the total membership actually increased, from 13,000 in 1941 to

16,000 in 1945 as more and more men discovered that service to one's country can best be rendered through organized effort.

During the years of World War Two there were no international conventions because of travel restrictions and the need for every Optimist to remain on the job till the war was won. Conferences were substituted for conventions to carry on the administrative work of the organization. The training of incoming club and district officers was made the responsibility of the district governors.

In the 1942 Wartime Conference the basic objectives of Optimism were reaffirmed: Friendship among Optimists, Optimism as a philosophy of life, patriotism and allegiance to good government and friendship with the boy.

It became apparent at this conference that their herculean war efforts had not been at the expense of the Optimists work with boys. Reports received revealed that the average amount of time and money per club devoted to boys work had increased throughout Optimist International. In view of this, conference delegates resolved that even more time should be devoted to club projects that contribute to the building of youth morals, citizenship and respect for law and order.

Long before the anxiously awaited arrival of V-E Day and V-J Day in 1945, those deliciously happy days that brought victory and an end to the fighting, Optimist International began its plan of action for the postwar years when it could resume its interrupted program of development, growth and effectiveness.

Although the curtailment of normal activities had resulted in Optimist International being in the best financial condition in its history, it faced the baffling problem of membership turnover. The average club was experiencing a turnover of around 25 percent, nearly twice that of normal times due at least in part to the unsettled conditions of nations at war.

To meet this problem Optimist International at its wartime conferences established a goal of 500 Life Memberships to provide for the postwar building of new clubs on solid foundations with thorough indoctrination of all new Optimists. By 1944 nearly 600 had been sold and the organization was insured a sound financial structure upon which to build when the war should end.

And with the dropping of the atomic bomb on Japan it was, at long last, all over. Optimists in uniform returned to their homes and civilian clothes. Those who had abandoned their careers to engage in war work were back at the old stand once more. Optimists everywhere turned from wartime projects to their own campaigns of enlarging and strengthening their organization through new members and new clubs. The record shows how successful they were.

It takes no more than a casual glance over the years to see that the organization has seen both "low moments" of struggle when only the most dedicated efforts of accomplished leaders kept Optimist International from "making progress backward" and "high moments" when giant strides were made forward. It is interesting to note that without exception its toughest times were caused by situations quite beyond its control—two World Wars and a vast economic depression—while its greatest acceleration came out of a favorable situation Optimist International itself had created.

Long time leaders of Optimist International who have both served and observed the organization agree that one of the "high moments" was the creation of the Life Membership Fund to provide proper financing for the building and indoctrination of new Optimist clubs.

They agreed, too, that another was the adoption of the club sponsorship program in 1950 in which Optimists went out and built new clubs themselves rather than leaving this important work in the hands of paid organizers.

Benefits of the club sponsorship plan are both many and obvious. The appearance of an Optimist, working voluntarily on his own time and often his own expense, is powerful evidence to a prospective Optimist that this indeed must be a worthy and worthwhile undertaking. By recruiting men for a new club in a neighboring community an Optimist can't help widening his circle of good men in that area. The friendship between the sponsoring club and the new club is bound to be stronger because of the keen interest developed during the club building program. These and other facts were learned in the early 1950s when Optimist International adopted the policy of growth by club sponsorship.

In those years Optimism spread at a rate never seen before in its history, from a little over 700 clubs in 1950 to more than 2400 in 1966.

Many of the longtime Optimists point to the creation of the Achievement and Awards program as a third "high moment." This system of laying down specific accomplishments for clubs, zones, districts and their officers and of recognizing properly those who achieve them was originated during the administration of George O. Browne of Indianapolis in 1950-1951 and activated the following year under the administration of Roly P. Nall of Los Angeles. In the years that have followed the stimulation given Optimist officers at all levels by the Achievement and Awards program has been invaluable to the over-all program.

While this program called for nothing revolutionary in the way of new duties and functions of Optimist officers it did provide a new level of excellence toward which they could work, a system by which they could measure their accomplishments and progress against those of others and a tangible award for those who served Optimism best.

One direct result of the growth of Optimist International during its "high moments" in its history was the need for larger and greater facilities for its International Office.

In the earliest days, the "office" of Optimist International could be carried around in a man's pocket or housed in one drawer of his desk. In 1919 the first "headquarters" was established in the secretary's office at 824 N. Pennsylvania Street in Indianapolis. Thirty months later it was moved to the Indiana College of Music and Fine Arts at 1410 N. Delaware Street in the same city. When the 1922 convention elected a San Francisco man as president, the International Office was moved there to his office at 354 Pine Street. Before the year was up both he and the office moved to 58 Sutter Street, San Francisco.

Delegates to the 1923 convention saw the impracticality of an international office that hopped about the country every year or two. They also realized the need for a secretary, a professional to devote full time to the needs of Optimist International.

They created such an office and set the first paid secretary, Thomas B. Elliott, up in business in St. Louis, at 816 Olive Street. Here, in one room, was established the organization's first real International Office. It remained there for a little more than a year before it was moved again, this time to the Railway Exchange Building, a structure that was to accommodate a constantly growing staff and its steadily enlarging facilities.

By 1955, with more than a thousand Optimist clubs and nearly 50,000 Optimists, it became obvious that the Office of Optimist International couldn't function much longer in a series of rooms scattered through several floors of an office building. The need for its own building, designed and constructed for the purpose, was growing greater. At the March, 1955, meeting of the International Board of Directors, Vice President William T. Tate, Dallas, Tex., urged the appointment of a fact-finding committee to investigate the possibilities of a new office building for Optimist International. The 1957 convention in Philadelphia saw the first positive step taken when delegates ordered establishment of a permanent headquarters building fund into which every Optimist would pay 50 cents semi-annually from January 1, 1958, until September 30, 1966.

A committee headed by William H. Pierce of Dallas, Tex., was given the responsibility of selecting a site and supervising design and construction of a new home of Optimist International. Serving with Bill Pierce were Harold W. Brand of Houston, Lucien L. Renuart, Miami, R. A. Harp, Philadelphia, Donald J. Twiss, M.D., of Toronto, and John W. Whatley of Atlanta. Others who served at various times on this committee were Dr. Francis J. Nash, Kansas City, Kan., Frank Baker, Austin, Tex., L. E. McKee, Long Beach, Calif., and Sydney R. Gee, London, Ont.

Two years were spent by the building committee in the survey of many cities in both the United States and Canada which had been proposed as a possible site for the new building. The committee finally settled on the city where the Office has been for nearly forty years, St. Louis, Mo.

The Indiana College of Music and Fine Arts in Indianapolis was the second location for the office of Optimist International. It was here for only six months when it was moved to San Francisco and then to St. Louis, where it has been since 1923. The present International Office building was occupied in February, 1962.

On Lindell Boulevard—long known as St. Louis' "Fifth Avenue" and at the turn of the century the most exclusive residential area in Missouri—the site was selected. Two handsome old mansions built in the 19th century were purchased and razed. On the 170 x 213 ft. lot Optimist International built its first International Office building, the first new construction in that neighborhood in decades and the first of many handsome, expensive and modern buildings that have been built there since.

The two story building provides 18,000 square feet of floor space, 14,000 devoted to office and work space and the rest to the board of directors' room, the conference room and the employees' lunch room.

Offices, light and airy, are built around vast areas of working space on both levels. Easily the most dramatic feature of the striking and attractive building is its main lobby, facing tree-lined Lindell Boulevard. Two levels high, it serves as a reception area for visitors. The receptionist's desk on a raised platform on the suspended stairway is easily accessible from either level.

On February 26, 1962, after weeks of preparation, the staff of Optimist International moved into its first permanent home. The Board of Directors held its first meeting in the new building the following month. Dedication ceremonies were held during the 1962 convention in St. Louis under the direction of International President Raymond R. Rembolt, M.D., of Iowa City, Iowa.

CHAPTER 10

By 1950 THE ROLE
of Optimist International as a leading force in the United States
and Canada in the field of boys work was well established and
widely known. Every community in which an Optimist club existed has seen the effect of the organization's time, money and
efforts that had been devoted willingly to the not unpleasant nor
unrewarding task of turning lively and restless boys into good
men and good citizens.

Familiar too, was the Optimists' method of operation and
their policies. No international or national project; none by districts or zones. The needs of boys vary from community to community and each individual Optimist club seeks out and tackles
the problem for the boys in its own vicinity. Strictly on the club
level, at the grass roots, are the boys work programs designed,
financed and carried out.

These individual projects range from large and costly boys'
homes, ranches, and farms to the individual attention and help

given one confused boy by one Optimist Uncle, from a fully equipped and staffed summer camp to the outfitting of one Boy Scout in a troop.

In 1950, 13 lads received some sort of attention for every Optimist on the rolls at an investment of $25.67 per man. That year 36,573 Optimists raised and spent $938,985 on 493,705 boys.

During the next few years more and more Optimists extended a helping hand to more and more boys, broadening their club projects to reach more youth, until in 1964, 35 boys got a boost for every Optimist at an expenditure of $47.30 per man. That year 80,565 Optimists spent $3,810,846 on 2,856,658 boys.

A portion of every Optimist's club dues goes directly into boys work, of course, but the great majority of funds spent in community service comes from the individual communities it benefits. Just as no two communities are exactly alike in their needs for boys so are no two alike when it comes to fund raising. What was a highly successful project in one city may be a total flop in another. Here, again, it is the business of the individual club to know its own community and to design its own programs for financing its boys work. Some clubs sell Christmas trees, others hold auctions. Some sponsor dances, parties, circuses and hobby shows while others are operating concession stands at fairs and sporting events. One Optimist is on the phone, taking orders from his friends for fruitcakes or light bulbs. Another has taken the day off, put on his old clothes and is having a wet but happy time at an Optimist Car Wash.

Optimist International, while it provides an almost unlimited supply of specific information and advice on fund raising, based on years of fact-finding and experience, plays no part in how the money raised from these club projects shall be spent other than to insist it all go to some public service in the community where it was raised. Activity reports submitted annually by the clubs reveal impressive totals in man-hours and money devoted to this vital program across the land.

The list of club-sponsored projects in boys work is almost .endless. Optimists provide the money—and often the supervision —for otherwise friendless lads in Boys' Clubs of America, in

Fund raising projects take many shapes. Top left photo: members of the Optimist Club of Saginaw, Mich., sold smiles and raised more than $2000; top right photo: the Optimist Club of Syracuse, N.Y., schedules an annual Shoe Shine Day and members man the stand in shifts; bottom photo: the Optimist Club of Manitowoc, Wis., auctioned a 1914 Ford for its money raising efforts.

Boy Scouts, in bowling clubs, in Junior Achievement, in drum and bugle corps, in rifle clubs and youth centers.

They conduct amateur talent shows, citizenship programs in schools and camps, roller derbies, contests and parades, driver training classes, football and baseball leagues, movie programs, safety patrols, science fairs and swimming parties.

They provide clothing for poor boys and unemployment bureaus for jobless ones. They finance exchange student programs and scholarship loan funds. They sponsor visual aid clinics and vocational guidance conferences.

Much of the Optimists' work with boys is done on Optimist owned property. Through the years the individual clubs have invested heavily in boys' homes, baseball parks, hot rod drag strips, ice skating rinks, swimming pools and day camps and lodges, until 1965 found their investment totaling nearly $11-million with almost $2-million more on the drawing boards for proposed construction.

Records show significant figures on how many men devoted how much time and how much money on how many boys, but they reveal but a small part of the story. The mind, the heart and the soul of a boy are far too complex and unfathomable to lend themselves to figures in a record book. Who can say, for example, exactly which or even how many youngsters were sufficiently impressed by an Optimist driver training course to accept safety on the road as a lifelong habit? To which lads among the many thousands who participate annually in the oratorical contest has the experience come as a glorious adventure of enough impact to set their eyes on new and greater goals?

In April of each year hundreds of Optimist clubs sponsor a Bike Safety Week. Every child with a bike is encouraged to bring it around for a safety inspection at no charge. Each is given a membership card in the Optimist Bike Safety Club and invited to take part in bike rodeos, parades and contests. During the week, too, the Optimists sponsor movies designed to inform the youngster in the safe operation of his bike and inspire him to safety habits. They conduct safety demonstrations and distribute safety literature.

Can any record book indicate how many youngsters have

avoided crippling accidents because of Bike Safety Week? Can anyone say how many lives this has saved?

Work with boys, as has been indicated, is an area for service that is without dimension. It does not concern itself exclusively with juvenile delinquents, as Optimists learned early. Ideally, it provides for every boy precisely what each boy needs, be it a home or the chance to race his bike against another's.

Among the millions of lads who have benefited from the efforts and devotion of Optimists, of course, only relatively few of them have required constant, around-the-clock attention. Actually, there aren't many homeless boys in the United States and Canada.

There are some, though, and many of these have found that necessary harbor in an Optimist home for boys. The majority of these lads cannot be classified as juvenile delinquents any more than one could fairly put that label on the teenagers who fought under George Washington in the American Revolution or who wore the blue or the grey in the American Civil War. They were rebels, too, in a way. They were rebelling against customs, codes and conventions of their day just as many young people do today.

Optimists consider these restless and often homeless youngsters to be potentially first class citizens who need nothing more than a good and influential friend, a normal supply of life's necessities and creature comforts, and the opportunity to discover for themselves that the good life is the only life.

In the 1920's Optimists in Los Angeles saw the need for proper housing and environment for boys who had no homes or whose homes provided less than the minimum requirements for the making of a healthy, decent adult citizen. They accepted the challenge and met it head-on. In the half century that has followed, the Optimist Home for Boys, now supported by Optimist clubs of Southern California, has been a haven for underprivileged youngsters. Entering as frightened, rebellious or merely bewildered lads, they have found in the Home more than food and shelter. They have been exposed, many for the first time in their young lives, to the normal program of boy development, to guidance, to the art of living with and respecting the rights of others, to good health and good attitudes. There is no yardstick by which one may measure the worth to society of the largest—and possibly the most successful—of these programs—The Optimist Home for Boys in Los Angeles.

A few years later, in San Antonio, a young clergyman named Don Holliman called the attention of his Optimist club to the appalling fact that homeless and neglected boys were sleeping under bridges and on park benches in the downtown area of the city. Investigation revealed that these were not "bad" boys but merely unwanted lads who, in many instances, had nowhere else to go at night. Obviously, unless someone held out a helping hand to them right away their circumstances would lead most, if not all of them, into serious trouble with the law.

With the help of other civic leaders, the Optimists got permission to use as a temporary home for these boys a fine old San Antonio residence that had long been vacant. This was the start of the now famous Boysville.

At first there were only a handful of boys in residence, most of them sent there by social workers and kindly policemen. But the effect of this radical change in environment was demonstrated dramatically by them. Increasing their efforts the Optimists launched a successful campaign for funds and bought the property. And before long Boysville was filled to overflowing. Forty-six boys was indeed a houseful, even for the old mansion.

Led by its five Optimist members, the board of directors of Boysville, made up of San Antonio's leading business and professional men, spearheaded another and greater drive. The work of Boysville in the area had not gone unnoticed and citizens of all economic levels gave generously. The result was the purchase of a new and larger property, this time 185 acres of good farm land about ten miles northwest of the city. Dormitories, offices and other facilities were built to accommodate 91 homeless boys.

San Antonio Optimists estimate that more than 700 lads have at one time or another been "citizens" of Boysville, sharing in the home and farm chores, engaging in sports, cultivating hobbies, enjoying entertainment and recreation, studying in their own library, governing themselves in a normal and well regulat-

The Optimist Home for Boys in Los Angeles, occupies five acres and includes ranch-type hillside buildings and a large physical education center.

Boysville in San Antonio, Tex., is supported in part by the Optimist Club of San Antonio. It covers 188 acres, including 78 acres of cultivable land.

ed life, and learning to assume the personal responsibilities required of every good citizen.

There are several such Optimist enterprises. Some are known as "Optimist Boys Ranch," "Optimist Boys Harbor" or simply "Optimist Home for Boys." In each one, throughout each year, boys of all races and creeds—or no creed at all—have found and are finding the good things in life that have been denied them through no fault of their own, good things that most of us accepted and took for granted as nothing more than part of the rights and privileges to which we were entitled.

Most of these establishments, naturally, are in larger metropolitan areas were the resources of several Optimist clubs may be drawn upon for support. In smaller cities and towns such permanent homes for boys are neither practical nor possible. In these areas the individual clubs turn their efforts toward other character building activities for their boys. The fundamental rule of "each club select its own most-needed project" has served Optimist International well indeed.

Once a year, however, all Optimism sets aside one week to recognize and commend the vast majority of teenagers who do not require special attention or help, those who are the leaders of their generation and those who do not stray from the prescribed route that leads to good adult citizenship.

This is now known throughout Canada and the United States as Youth Appreciation Week.

The whole idea was born on a bitter cold winter night near the foothills of the Blue Ridge Mountains in North Carolina, on an icy, hazardous road running 70 miles between the small town of Morganton and Charlotte. Optimist T. Earl Yarborough and his wife were driving back home to Charlotte after Earl's assistance in the organization of a Junior Optimist club in Morganton. The drive under normal conditions would have required less than two hours. Tonight, on the glazed roads, it took five and the Yarboroughs had ample time to talk and to reflect on the incidents of the evening.

"It beats me," said Earl. "On a night like this every one of those kids showed up for the meeting. Some of them had to walk

State governors and mayors proclaim Youth Appreciation Week every year. Here the mayor of Salt Lake City signs the proclamation for the Optimist Club of Salt Lake City for the first Youth Appreciation Week in 1957.

The Optimist Club of New Orleans sponsored, in 1957, a Youth in Government day, when young people from the various schools took over the executive offices of the city. Here the mayor of New Orleans turns over the gavel to his young substitute.

several miles, I understand. They must be pretty good kids to be so enthusiastic over their new Junior Optimist club."

Then, almost as an afterthought, he added, "I wonder what the morning papers will have to say about this. Nothing, in all probability, for it's really not great news. If those boys had been arrested for swiping hubcaps or cutting tires or something, though, there would have been a story about that."

It was a real shame, the Yarboroughs agreed, that so much public attention is paid to teenagers who go wrong and so little to those who stay right. After all, 95 percent of our young people never see a policeman except to wave a friendly greeting to him as they drive by. Should they not be recognized publicly and commended? Do they not deserve at least a pat on the back?

By the time he reached his home Earl had the conviction that such a gesture by Optimists should, could and must be given. He armed himself with statistics on juvenile delinquency and on juvenile decency. He solicited the aid of two fellow Optimists, Harold Smoak and a Charlotte newspaperman, Kays Gary. He carried his idea for a Youth Appreciation Day to his own Optimist club and to the North Carolina statehouse. With enthusiastic endorsement of Governor Luther Hodges, the success of the project was assured.

Radio stations, newspapers, civic clubs, teachers, parents, youth and church leaders, public officials . . . all were captivated by this new, dramatic and positive approach to the matter of teenager behavior. On May 22, 1955, North Carolina observed the first Youth Appreciation Day and it was an overwhelming success.

Optimist International, of course, watched the birth and development of the idea closely. Here was a program that had come along at just the right time, one that promised to change the attitude of the adult world from "what's the matter with our young people?" to "how splendid are the vast majority of our teenagers!"

The following year, 1956, Optimist International scheduled a Youth Appreciation Week program on a pilot basis in five states and one Canadian province. North Carolina, of course, was one of the five. Acceptance of the program and eager participation in it were reported from every trial area.

In the autumn of 1957 Optimist International launched for the first time in history a continent-wide program that had as its sole purpose the recognition, commendation and encouragement of the 95 percent of all teenagers whose feet are firmly planted on the right track and from whose midst will come the adult leaders of tomorrow's world.

That year saw more than a thousand such programs sponsored by Optimist clubs. The number increased steadily until in 1965 more than 1900 Optimist clubs gave the young people of their communities a well deserved "Pat on the Back."

CHAPTER 11

IN SEPTEMBER 1926
the Optimist magazine pointed with pride to the fact that it had
been published regularly for six years and that "never has an
article been printed in the publication that would lower the high
standard of the Optimist movement."

Three months earlier the publicity committee had come to the
international convention armed with some constructive suggestions regarding the magazine's make-up and material. Most of
these proposals were good and remained in effect two or more
years. One, however, was a resounding dud. The committee recommended that a fiction department be added and launched
with a serial mystery.

The advice was well taken and the next issue brought to Optimists "The Maxwell Mystery" by Carolyn Wells. For some reason not now known the serial was dropped "just at the most
exciting part" and how the mystery turned out is still for those
Optimist magazine readers a mystery.

With this one exception the Optimist magazine has, since the year following the organization of Optimist International, been the main source of information about Optimism for all Optimists. It is the one vital link between every club member and Optimist International. It was first published in Indianapolis. For two years it was published in Philadelphia, edited there by the "director of publicity." In 1928 the magazine's home was returned to the International Office, now in St. Louis, and there it has remained.

It was through the magazine that most Optimists learned of the constantly changing pattern of Optimist districts as the organization grew.

At the first convention in Louisville in 1919, delegates authorized creation of seven districts or "sections," each to be overseen by a governor who would also serve on the international board of governors. In 1922 the International Optimist Club— then only in the United States—was divided into 14 districts. Two years later a 15th was added, the entire nation of Canada! In that year also, Dayton, Ohio, was the scene of the first district convention. Delegates from the 15 clubs in District Five assembled, traveling from the far corners of Indiana, Ohio and Michigan.

For many years Optimist districts were identified by number and, as more and more new clubs came into being, district boundaries were changed from year to year. In 1963 identification of districts by number was abandoned and names were introduced. In the more thickly populated areas and where Optimist clubs are many, district boundaries are drawn along state or province lines and the district is identified by the state or province name. In other areas where the Optimist district extends over parts of several states or provinces, a combination name is given or one identifying that particular area.

As Optimism continues to grow there will be more changes in the district picture, as districts draw toward state and provincial lines and encompass more and more zones and clubs.

From their magazine, members learned also about the constant growth of Optimist International and additions to their International staff, which has grown from a one-man, brief case office to a multi-department storehouse of ideas and experiences headed by specialists in every field of service club administration. Now there are nearly 50 men and women who enter the front door of the International Office every day to review, analyze and coordinate the thousands of reports, bulletins and other informative and inquiring letters, which arrive daily from Optimists and Optimist clubs everywhere. The information gathered from this voluminous source is funneled back to clubs to provide them with more know-how in all phases of club operation. The magazine also informed members of the resignation of Russell F. Meyer, for 25 years their International secretary-treasurer, on December 31, 1953, and the appointment of Bernard B. Burford to that office the following May.

Following the 1963 convention Optimists not in attendance learned from their magazine of the creation of a new department within Optimism, a new, broad area of service that was open for them. In Toronto the delegates had authorized the appointment of a Community Service Committee, the creation of a Community Service Department at the International Office and the engaging of a professional to direct it.

Though the department was new, Optimists were no strangers to community service. Just as the men who put together the organization called Optimist International soon learned there were greater rewards in boys work than in mere business reciprocity, so did they also learn that, admirable and sorely needed though it be, boys work alone should not have an exclusive right to all the service a good Optimist club can perform.

A part of Optimist International's objective is "to promote an active interest in good government and civic affairs, to inspire respect for law, to promote patriotism and work for international accord and friendship among all people."

From the beginning Optimist clubs have busied themselves effectively in their communities with civic improvement projects, with fire prevention, with citizenship programs, safety campaigns, get-out-the-vote drives and public health promotions. When you find an organized effort being made in a community toward its own betterment, chances are you'll find an Optimist club involved in it wholeheartedly if not at the bottom of it.

One of the earliest, most spectacular and successful community betterment projects was sparked and quarterbacked by an Asheville, North Carolina, Optimist of perhaps humble economic station—he drove a laundry wagon—but of flaming civic spirit and extraordinary powers of organization.

Before 1907 only a few hardy mountain climbers knew of the beauty of a natural forest of rhododendron, mountain laurel and mountain azelea that grew rampant atop rugged old Craggy Mountain, a few miles from Asheville. Then two local nature enthusiasts blazed a foot trail to the top and encouraged their friends to make the arduous climb. The riotous display of color that burst upon them when they made it was worth the effort but for 20 years the natural gardens remained unknown to most of Asheville people and to practically all visitors.

In 1931, with the depression in full swing, Asheville was feeling keenly the loss of the tourist trade it had so long considered part of its normal economy. While leaders were casting about for a new attraction which could be acquired without undue expenditure Optimist James A. Ware brought forth his plan.

He personally was well acquainted with the floral wonders of Craggy Mountain for he had climbed the trail almost every weekend for years. He also had seen the world famous Magnolia Gardens in Charleston and the beauty spots of renown in Colorado.

"But," he addressed his Optimist club, "when the rhododendron, the azelea and the laurel are in bloom on old Craggy there is nothing in the United States to compare with it."

Such an attraction should be brought within easy reach of everyone, tourist and resident alike, he insisted. And now was the time to move as Congress was rushing through emergency road measures and other acts for the relief of the unemployment.

His club appointed him a committee of one to represent the Optimists in an effort to form an Inter-Club Committee to bring to bear the full force of all service clubs on the project. Other Optimists were named to take up with public and private groups the proposition to build a road to the top of Craggy Mountain.

Practically everyone in Asheville, from the mayor to the barbershop bootblack, during the next few weeks took the hike up the mountain trail, inspired by the publicity attending Jimmy Ware's Optimist campaign. The project, as a result, was accepted and for the next few years several hundred CCC boys enjoyed healthful and profitable employment as well as fun in building the first automobile highway up to the beautiful wildflower gardens on the mountain top.

Jimmy Ware died in 1936 but Craggy Rhododendron Gardens remain after him as one of the South's most popular attractions and an everlasting monument to an Optimist with far-reaching ideas and the unquenchable enthusiasm to see them through.

As it was with the Asheville Optimists, so it is with hundreds of other clubs. They have been at this business of community service for many years. Some projects are like theirs, requiring several years to accomplish and then remaining on as an asset to the community long after those responsible have passed away.

Others are of a temporary nature, as during the great Ohio River flood of 1937 when Optimist clubs in cities along its banks conducted organized campaigns for the relief of flood victims. Or during World War Two when Optimists involved themselves in every public effort to win the war, as reported earlier.

In addition to the efforts expended in this field by the individual clubs, Optimist International has originated several effective continent-wide programs, unifying Optimists of the United States and Canada into a strong force for public good.

One of the first of these, launched and pursued years before the creation of the Community Service Department, was the organization of an all-out campaign against the illegal sale and use of narcotics, especially among young people.

At the 36th annual convention of Optimist International in June, 1954, in Houston, delegates passed a resolution asking all Optimists and Optimist clubs to urge legislation for more severe penalties against the illegal sale of narcotics. From that time on Optimists have campaigned vigorously by warning legislators and citizens of increasing drug addiction. Optimists have recognized the crime of selling narcotics to minors as equal in magnitude to the crimes of murder and kidnaping. At the 1955 convention in Montreal, Optimists endorsed the death penalty for the conviction of an illegal narcotics sale to a juvenile.

Legislation called for in the resolution adopted at the two Optimist conventions was enacted by Congress in 1956. The bill greatly strengthened narcotics regulations by permitting juries to recommend the death penalty for anyone who sells or gives heroin to children under 18 and all penalties for narcotics law violations were drastically increased.

Legislation, however, is not the full answer, as Past International President Walter A. Reiling, M.D., of Dayton points out. The complete answer must come out of a long and hard-fought campaign of public education, proper care and medical treatment within the reach of all addicted, activating of a narcotics squad in every state and province and compulsory treatment for every known addict.

The Optimists' war on the illegal sale and use of narcotics is already an old one. Some advances have been made. Others will come and yet others until the evil is under control. Optimists never quit.

About the same time the Optimists looked with horror on the illegal uses of narcotics and what they were doing to the bodies of our young people, they resolved to wage a similar campaign against another evil that was assailing the minds of children to an alarming degree, the evil of pornography.

One out of every 35 children of school age, estimates the United States Post Office Inspection Service, receives at least one item of pornographic filth each year in the family mailbox. In the great majority of cases the material has not been ordered by the child. His name and address wound up on the mailing lists of smut peddlers through an innocent purchase of some legitimate mail-order merchandise. The volume of this traffic in mail-order obscenity has risen alarmingly. It doubled over a recent five year period and the Post Office believes that unless it is checked by public action it will again double in the near future.

Optimist International for several years has been taking this action. Its Anti-Smut Campaign material is available to all Optimist clubs at all times. The packet contains step-by-step information on how a club may alert its community to the evil that is being spread by mail throughout the land.

Club resolutions, speakers' bureaus, public meetings, newspaper and radio publicity, all are designed with one purpose in mind, to alert parents to the seriousness of the situation and to solicit their help in putting it down. Parents are urged to be on the lookout for such pornographic materials in their own mailboxes and, if any is discovered, to forward it at once to their local Post Office.

Still another social problem in the modern community is that of the school drop-out. Again, Optimist International through its clubs has organized and activated a program of positive action to meet it. Many Optimists have engaged personally in the Stay-in-School program through service on committees which meet with school officials and youth leaders and then with the young people themselves to encourage them to continue their education and to offer any assistance needed to remain in school.

One of the first and most dramatic projects to come out of Optimist International's new Community Service Committee was the now widely publicized Respect for Law program. It has been undertaken in an effort to combat apathy toward crime and the dispensation of justice.

Perhaps the most shocking example of the apparently growing attitude of "I don't want to get involved" came from the streets of New York where a young woman was brutally attacked and murdered even though 40 persons heard her screams but not one would lift a finger to help her, not even to call the police.

Incensed by this and other similar incidents in the news daily, Optimists demanded an organized counter-action. Many months of study and planning went into the campaign. Co-operation of both the Federal Bureau of Investigation and the Royal Canadian Mounted Police was asked for and received. At last the program was fully developed.

Optimist International's Respect for Law program has three basic objectives:

To combat public apathy and indifference toward crime and criminals and rekindle proper respect for and moral responsibility under the law,

Newspaper reporter Don Dust, left, and East Orange, N.J., Mayor James Kelly, center, receive medallions from Robert J. Buchanan, president of the Optimist Club of East Orange, N.J.

Les Bell, left, vice president of the Optimist Club of Portsmouth, Va., presents medallion to Gunner's Mate Dennis Denham.

Lois Stone, second from left, and Mrs. Marion Renner, receive citations from Donald M. Winter, left, president of the Optimist Club of Rocky Mountain, Denver, Colo. in the presence of Colorado-Wyoming District Governor James L. Roffe.

To encourage, promote and recognize the participation of the public in the dispensation of justice, through service as witnesses and on juries, and co-operation with law enforcement officials in the discharge of their duties, and

To better acquaint the public with the duties, responsibilities, and needs of law enforcement officials and to recognize and honor unusual, outstanding services rendered by citizens, including law enforcement officers.

It is not the intent of Optimist International to encourage citizens to become martyrs or vigilantes. It does not propose that individuals should risk their lives or their personal safety by attempting to forestall the commission of a crime or to apprehend a criminal. But it does urge an attack on the freedom with which criminals operate and on the failure of citizens to assume their responsibilities in the matter of law enforcement.

While the work of inspiring and educating citizens young and old to Respect the Law goes on quietly but effectively, the program does contain one facet that many times has drawn public attention, often in a quite spectacular manner.

It is the Optimist International Respect for Law Citation, a handsome medallion honoring any citizen of the United States or Canada who voluntarily becomes involved in the business of keeping law and order regardless of personal hazards or risk of physical harm.

A few examples:

When Billy Brice, 45, of Austin, Tex., awoke that September morning in 1965, he had no hint that it would be anything other than one more day of his normal, daily routine. Before it ended, however, he had voluntarily become mixed up in an incident that might well have resulted in his being seriously injured or even killed.

Billy observed a police officer being attacked by one of two prisoners he was taking into custody. Instead of watching the action from a safe distance or turning his head and walking away—as all too many other citizens would have done—Billy rushed to the officer's aid. He helped him subdue the recalcitrant prisoner and then remained by the policeman's side until complete control of the situation had been achieved.

All 13 Optimist clubs in Austin joined in nominating Billy for the Respect for Law Citation. The nomination was approved by Optimist International and the first citation was awarded to Billy Brice of Austin, Texas, in December, 1965.

The second medallion was awarded not long after, on recommendation of the Optimist Club of Bluffton, Ind. A citizen of nearby Ossian, Ind., 25-year-old David Brookmeyer, singlehandedly apprehended an armed fugitive who he later discovered was wanted for murder in California.

As the months passed Optimist clubs across the land reported a stream of examples of exemplary citizenship and personal heroism. In Prince Albert, Sask., 12-year-old Billy Dewhurst went with his father to investigate a burglary. When the intruder was discovered the lad leaped in and physically helped his father apprehend the suspect.

Active good citizenship, the Optimists were to learn quickly, knows no age limits. An 81-year-old woman was cited for bravery after she had observed three youths attacking a cab driver in front of her home. She rushed out with her shotgun and nipped that crime-in-the-making in its tracks. Again, three boys, 11, 12 and 13, chased a suspected shoplifter an hour on their bikes, despite threats of injury or possible assault. One dropped off the chase to notify police and the suspect was arrested.

From every corner of Optimist International have come nominations for the Respect for Law Citation, each based on incidents such as those mentioned here. In each instance when the nomination was approved, the presentation has been made in the recipient's home community by the nominating Optimist club or clubs. Attended by excellent publicity locally, the incident does more than pay tribute to a citizen who has demonstrated respect for law. It also points up the value of every citizen's interest in and concern for the maintenance of law and order, and the efforts of Optimists everywhere to increase its activity.

Respect for Law medallions may be and are awarded to citizens at any time. By the time of the organization's Golden Anniversary convention in Louisville in 1968, more than 250 had been presented. In less than five years—by 1972—that number had reached 500.

These, plus literally thousands of others who have shown respect for law in less dramatic ways, have learned from the Optimist program one irrefutable fact—That most citizens are indeed involved in the enforcement of the laws of his land whether he will admit it—or wants to be—or not.

Civilization . . . . . Society . . . . . Government . . . . . All are everyone's personal business.

The situation was well expressed many years ago:

"Any man's death diminishes me, because I am involved in mankind; and therefore never send to know for whom the bell tolls; it tolls for thee."

CHAPTER 12

ASK ANY OPTIMIST
who has ever attended one and he will tell you that the high
point of every Optimist year is the International convention.
For the better part of a week each year since 1919, Optimists
have come from far flung points to meet again old friends, make
new ones and, working together, to advance even further the
programs and the principles of the organization.

Through the passing years they have so assembled in most of
the major cities of the United States and Canada. From the ad-
dresses by men and women of international fame and prestige
they have drawn inspiration; from exhibits, reports and work-
shop sessions they have been informed and stimulated to return
to their home clubs determined to work with even more devotion
toward even "greater achievements of the future."

International conventions are especially impressive and important to newly elected club and district officers. Here they at-
tend the vital training sessions in which the fundamentals of

leadership are examined in detail and the proper and effective administration of a good Optimist club is spelled out, step by step. Here most club presidents-elect for the first time get the "big picture" and come to full realization of just how great and worthwhile is Optimist International.

Every session, every ceremony is deeply impressive. The eyes of the first-timer are opened widest for the total concept, however, at those in which Optimist International is recognized and commended by other prestigious organizations for its effective work in its many areas of service to others. The list of such honors and commendations received by Optimist International through the years is long indeed, much too long to be included here in its entirety. Here are but a few examples to indicate their worth and their importance:

The Babe Ruth League Citation,
The National Sheriffs Association Citation,
The Sertoma Citation for Fifty Years of Service to Mankind,
The National Police Officers Association Citation,
The American Heritage Foundation's Award for Outstanding Performance,
The Crusade for Freedom Distinguished Service Award,
The Boys' Clubs of America Golden Anniversary Award,
The National Safety Council Award for Outstanding Contributions to Highway Safety,
The American Society of Association Executives' Award of Merit,
The Bicycle Institute's Public Service Award,
The Office of Civil Defense Mobilization's Certificate of Appreciation,
The U. S. Treasury Department's 20th Anniversary Savings Bond Award,
The Civil Air Patrol's Cadet Program Citation, and
The Girl Scouts of America's Plaque for Outstanding Service.

Not all of the organization's achievements however are recognized and commended on the convention floor. Indeed, some of its highest moments have come at other times and in other places.

You have read in an earlier chapter of the birth and develop-

Nicholas C. Mueller, right, 1959-60 president of Optimist International accepts the 1960 Public Service Award from the president of the Bicycle Institute of America, H. W. Huffman, Jr. The presentation took place at the 42nd Annual Convention in Grand Rapids, Mich.

A certificate of appreciation for outstanding service to civil defense was presented to 1960-61 president of Optimist International, John W. Whatley, right, by Hugh Van Epps of the Office of Civil Defense at the 43rd Annual Convention of Optimist International in Las Vegas, Nev.

At the 45th Annual Convention of Optimist International in Toronto, Secretary-Treasurer Bernard B. Burford, left, was presented with a replica of the Liberty Bell by Thomas L. Husselton, of the U.S. Savings Bond Division of the U.S. Treasury Department.

Also at the Toronto convention, President John M. Grimland, Jr., accepted a George Washington Honor Medal from Kenneth D. Wells, II, of the Freedoms Foundation.

ment of one of the finest programs—Youth Appreciation Week. Its high water mark came in 1971.

On July 2 of that year the United States Congress by joint resolution passed Public Law 92-43. It designated the week beginning the following November 8 as Youth Appreciation Week. The resolution also requested the President to issue a proclamation calling for the observance of that week.

And so it was done. On November 5, in the Oval Room of the White House, President Richard M. Nixon signed the first Youth Appreciation Week Proclamation in the presence of Immediate Past President Charles C. Campbell, Optimist T. Earl Yarborough, the originator of the Youth Appreciation Week concept, sponsors of the bill in both Houses of Congress and 21 young people from 12 states who represented the youth of today.

Speaking informally with these exceptional young citizens the President said, "I would say to you this is an exciting time to be alive."

He commended them for what they were and what they stood for. He challenged all youth to prepare themselves to be leaders in the world that lies ahead of them. He urged them as the first generation to have the opportunity to enjoy a full generation of peace to "build a compassionate world."

The pen with which President Nixon signed the first Youth Appreciation Week Proclamation is today proudly displayed among other trophies of success and accomplishment in the Past President's room at the Optimist International office building in St. Louis.

Now back to the International convention. . . .

It is here that Optimists chart their course for the coming year. Resolutions brought before the delegates are examined carefully and debated thoroughly, often with considerable articulation and vigor. It is here that Optimists select the members who will serve on the International Board of Directors the following administrative year.

With the exception of the World War II years, when affairs of the organization were administered through war-time conferences, there has always been on the convention agenda plenty of time for entertainment, sight seeing and informal good fellowship. There is fun for everyone, from the tiniest toddler to the oldest Optimist. International conventions are family affairs.

Entertainment highlight for Optimists is their annual fun favorite, the "Old Timers Breakfast," featuring a program of hilarity and the traditional and now famous Optimist Countdown, inaugurated in 1933 by Optimist Maury Walsh of Birmingham, Ala. All present are asked to stand at their places at the breakfast table. Those for whom it is their first convention are asked to be seated, then who are attending for the second time, then the third and so on until there are but a handful of Old Timers who have attended every convention since " 'way back when."

But still the countdown goes on. At last there remains on his feet but one Optimist out of the hundreds in the room. As you might well expect, the tribute paid the "Oldest Old Timer" is both thunderous and prolonged.

There's another traditional event on each convention slate, although it is attended by a much smaller group. This is the annual Past Presidents' Luncheon. Here the former leaders of Optimist International gather together to appraise the current status of their organization, to re-live both the high and low moments of the past and to receive into the ranks of the Elder Statesmen the retiring president of Optimist International. Here, in one room, are assembled the men who among them can point to literally hundreds of years of labor for and devotion to an organization in which they have so long and wholeheartedly believed.

After the convention proper has been adjourned, a third group of Optimists remain for a serious and arduous session of work. These are the governors-designate of Optimist districts who within a short time will assume the responsibility and duties of district leadership and administration.

Every phase of the Optimist program is gone into in great detail. All projects, old and new, are examined thoroughly. Every facet of leading an Optimist district is explored in depth. During the training sessions, during which both veteran Optimist leaders and members of the professional staff are heard, the governors-designate begin to comprehend the long range planning, the careful preparations and the behind-the-scenes work that have gone into the program that has made their organization what it is today. They also begin to be aware of what it will be

The social event of the annual convention of Optimist International for the ladies is the Ladies' Luncheon.

A highlight of every international convention is the Old Timers' Breakfast, originated in 1933 by Maurice M. Walsh, Birmingham, Ala. At the 1964 convention President George Cobley left, presented **Maury with a commemorative plaque.**

tomorrow.

When they depart these men are fully equipped with the tools and the stimulation it will take to organize their district's efforts, to instruct their lieutenant governors and to inspire Optimist clubs and Optimists to reach even higher plateaus of accomplishment and service.

Some of the programs so new to district and club officers are almost as old as the organization itself. The work with boys, as we have seen, began in its earliest years, to cite but one example.

Each year, however, as more is learned from practical experience, old programs are re-evaluated and up-dated and new ones introduced. For instance, the oratorical contest which had been conducted pretty much along the same lines for decades, was revamped in 1971 and broadened to include competition among girls as well as boys. The competition ends at the district level, rather than at the International Convention, and the winners of the 39 district contests receive scholarships of not less than $500 each.

Other programs have been recently launched. The year 1968-69 saw the advent of Operation Reach Out, a co-operative effort coordinated by the Office of Economic Opportunity, and Partners in Service, a joint program with the Boy Scouts of America. The following year found Optimist clubs busy with other innovations. And each succeeding year brought more opportunities for even greater and more varied service.

Some of the programs adopted were designed to inspire and to recognize the achievements of individual Optimists and those of Optimist clubs in strengthening their own organization. A few examples:

The 1966-67 administration under Robert H. Leonard saw the introduction of the International President's Golden Circle. It was the first internationally sponsored program to recognize the achievements of men at work in and for their own clubs. It has been awarded to Optimists who have been more than casually interested and involved in their club's activities.

International President Norman Shipley (1971-72) introduced "The President's Mug" as a trophy for those active in the sponsorship of new Optimist members.

The Friend of Youth award program, introduced under the

administration of Dr. Carl L. Bowen (1964-65), put the spotlight on clubs engaged in conducting organized activities for the youth of tomorrow.

These and other such programs were designed and activated not for the sole and somewhat selfish purpose of making the Optimist organization merely bigger and busier, however. Their ultimate goal was to make it greater and, thus, to contribute even more to the advancement of the good life and the well-being of the people of the United States and Canada. Service to these people, of all ages and in all walks of life, is, when you get to the heart of it, what the organization is all about.

To organize and channel this unified and devoted effort, several worthwhile programs have been developed. None was the result of an hour or two of casual exchange of ideas in a committee meeting or at a single session of the International Board of Directors. Each is the result of many hours of study, research and consultation with recognized experts in specific areas. Some of them were several years in the incubation stage before their activation.

Optimists first heard, for instance, of Project RSVP at their 1968 convention in Bal Harbour, Fla. This was pointed out in his annual report by Executive Secretary Hugh H. Cranford as "as worthy an endeavor as any ever undertaken by our organization." He explained it like this:

"The individual letters in RSVP refer to the need for citizens to REGISTER, STUDY, VOTE and PARTICIPATE. The primary objective is to renew and stimulate public interest, faith and participation in the government; to indicate that the problems in government today are not in the basic system but in the lack of active citizen interest and involvement in the process of making the elective system work."

Optimists in the ensuing year tackled another grave challenge, that of renewing their fight against drug abuse. Its revitalized Drug Abuse Information Program was developed in cooperation with the American Medical Association and outlined the steps to be taken by Optimist clubs in working with local doctors, druggists and law enforcement officials in attacking the problem.

During the 1971 convention in Minneapolis the International Board approved the Tri-Star Basketball Program for boys 8 to

13 years of age. This was a natural for both the lads and the sponsoring Optimist clubs. It had its origin in Dayton, Ohio, in 1968 when the Riverdale Optimist club of that city conducted a Pass, Shoot and Dribble Contest for boys. From that first contest, entered into with such enthusiasm by men and boys alike, growth of the program was nothing short of phenomenal. Optimist International was alert to its potential and, after a few legal difficulties were worked out, re-organized the program a bit and presented it as an opportunity for all clubs.

The first year of Tri-Star competition saw more than 300 clubs and something like 75,000 youngsters participating in exciting activity. Competing with others of their own age, boys demonstrated their skills at passing, shooting and dribbling. Some of the contests were held as half-time entertainment for spectators at high school, college and professional basketball games. Handsome trophies were awarded the winners and countless thousands saw Optimists at work under their original motto, "Friend of the Boy." It is easy to understand why this particular program has grown each year since its inception.

Optimist International has long been aware of the many problem areas that cloud the horizons of today's teenagers. It has also recognized the fact that young men and women in senior high schools should have both a voice and a hand in seeking ways of correcting them.

In 1972 the Opportunity for Involvement Club program, designed specifically to meet this need, was adopted. To state it briefly, an Opportunity for Involvement Club of young men and women in the 10th, 11th and 12th grades (the upper four grades in Canada) serves as a vehicle through which they may become active and involved in solving problems that challenge their community and society.

Though each club is sponsored by an Optimist club which suggests certain guidelines for its activities, both the operation of the OI Club and its programs are in the hands of the young members themselves. Service projects, social activities and fund raising events are many and varied but each serves a twofold purpose—each results in a better society and each provides an exercise in good citizenship for young men and women who care enough to want to become involved in striving to achieve it.

"Ecology" is a word that has been in every standard dictionary for years. It has been only in recent years, however, that it has emerged into the popular vernacular. This is because the average citizen has come only lately to realize that something has been happening to his environment that never happened before and that "something" is serious, perhaps even tragic. It is called pollution.

Even as this crisis began to emerge, Optimist International was devising a program to combat it. While no one man, nor single club nor even the whole of Optimist International can hope to put an end to all pollution, Optimists can and do provide a concrete program by which towns, cities and nations may meet the challenge.

The program is called L-I-F-E—Living is for Everything and was unveiled at the convention in Montreal.

Again, here is an Optimist program through which a club may educate, stimulate and lead its home community in an organized battle for clean air, pure water, uncluttered streets, proper disposal of trash and junk, a quiet atmosphere—in short, the natural, healthful, serene and unspoiled environment that was here before the coming of what is now referred to with a wry laugh as "civilization."

On Sunday, October 15, 1972, there arrived in St. Louis 70 of North America's top community leaders, hand-picked for their prestige, expertise at getting things done and their painful awareness of a mounting social problem.

They had come at the request of Optimist International for a two-day seminar, financed by a grant of $20,000 by the United States government, to consider that problem and what could be done about it. The Surgeon General of United States Public Health Service, Jesse L. Steinfeld, M.D., had summed it up succinctly in a letter to all Optimists:

"The venereal disease epidemic," he wrote, "has spread to every corner of our nation. No city, no neighborhood can afford to ignore this danger to the health of its citizens. Claiming a victim—usually a young person—every 15 seconds, it has become the most threatening communicable disease in the United States."

Optimist International, with the launching of its program,

AVOID, in 1972, became one of the first service club organizations to move in a direction to conduct an active program to combat syphilis and gonorrhea.

Optimists, as all thinking citizens, are quite aware that venereal diseases lie in a most socially sensitive area. They normally are not discussed in polite society. Victims of VD feel that they are not socially acceptable. They are also aware that because of the stigma society has attached to VD, any young person who suspects he or she might be infected is highly reluctant to seek out medical confirmation and, if needed, medical assistance.

These factors, plus the fact that many secondary schools teach nothing about VD, are in great measure responsible for the burgeoning epidemic. It is in this vital area that the Optimists' AVOID program centers its efforts. Working in close cooperation with medical, health, social and educational agencies, they seek to expose the hush-hush aura of mystery that surrounds venereal diseases, to present to today's youth the simple, true facts and to stem the epidemic wave through public information.

CHAPTER 13

WHAT MIGHT WELL HAVE BEEN
Optimist International's greatest moment in the spotlight of
public attention came on New Year's Day, 1968.

Hundreds of thousands lined the streets of Pasadena, Calif.,
to see the famous Tournament of Roses Parade. Literally millions more on the North American continent watched it on
television. Among the more than 60 beautiful and lavish floats
making up the parade was one of more than casual interest to
Optimists everywhere.

As it passed them in the stands or across the television screen,
everyone smiled or chuckled. To many it gave a hearty laugh.
It was a huge float of complicated design and elaborate construction, but it carried only one single theme—the glorious
pleasures of boyhood. It consisted of a single figure, that of a
typical kid, floating on his back in the "ol' swimmin' hole."
Perched on one bare big toe was a frog, obviously enjoying the
fun with the youngster. The feelings of the lad—and those of

123

President (1967-68) of Optimist International William R. Newhouse and Mrs. Newhouse and the Tournament of Roses Parade float "Ooooohh Boy," sponsored by Optimist International in the 1968 event.

everyone who looked upon it and remembered—were expressed by the two words that appeared across the sole of one bare foot rising above the water: "OOOOOOHH BOY!"

Fourteen awards are made by the judges who examine and evaluate the entries. One of the major awards is the Judges' Special Award for Humor. To the delight of Optimists everywhere—and especially the many California Optimists who had labored so long and hard—the 1968 award went to Optimist International!

The International Float Committee was headed by Vinnie Simpson, past distinguished governor of the Pacific Southwest District. Past International President George Cobley supervised the finances and maintained liaison between the West Coast and the International Office. Literally dozens of other Optimists and friends of the organization gave liberally of their time, talents and energies; many of them working day and night through the final week before deadline to complete the task on time.

The impact of the prize-winning float upon the crowds who saw it and the impression it made upon the judges were nothing short of terrific.

True, it is that money and long hours of labor were spent to create the "Ooooohh Boy!" float that could have but one fleeting moment of glory in the sun, but the beneficial results will remain for months, even years to come.

It was an undertaking bold in its inception and creative in its completion, one that will be long remembered as the highly successful achievement that drew the attention of all North America to the good work of Optimist International.

It is significant to note that less than a month before the Optimist float drew international attention in Pasadena, another tangible symbol of Optimism was unveiled before the International Office in St. Louis. Not constructed of wire, light plastic and paper to last but a day, this symbol was carved out of sheer granite to stand for as long as there is Optimism anywhere in the world.

It is a sculptured art form conceived and created by the internationally known sculptor, William Conrad Severson, of St. Louis, to stand as Optimism's "Symbol of Service." Standing

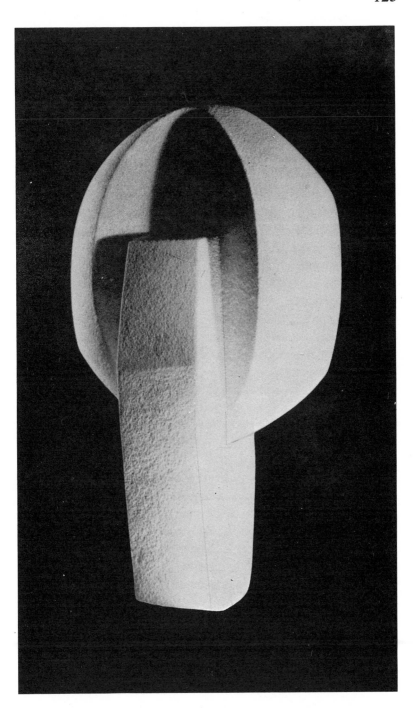

eight and one-half feet tall and weighing six tons, the sculpture is the designer's conception of the "O" and the "I" of Optimist International. It was sculpted from a single piece of off-white granite quarried near Barre, Vt., and mounted on a square base of polished black granite from Quebec.

In his remarks as master of ceremonies at the dedicatory service on December 8, 1967, Past President Cobley recalled it had been 19 years since delegates to an International convention voted to construct a headquarters building and noted that final landscaping details, due the following spring, would, with the addition of the granite symbol, complete the project.

Later, in speaking of his work, sculptor Severson said, "Artists design and make beautiful, but symbols are evidence of a far deeper involvement of men. The artist is incident to, or means of, their articulation. The sculpture I have carved . . . . . . is decidedly symbolic.

"It is designed to be beautiful, but just how individuals respond to that beauty is incidental to its purpose. As in all works of art, I would anticipate divergence of opinion.

"It is of the essence that consideration and value be understood as symbolic and that individuals respond personally, out of the context of their backgrounds of experience. Like and dislike are but phases of establishing relationship.

"If controversy ensues, it is desirable because it requires personal identification to argue."

Mr. Severson explained that granite was chosen for its allusion to strength and permanence; white granite for its pure and noble associations, black granite to provide emphasis for the white.

"Where the 'O' and the 'I' was the origin of the concept," he continued, "it is far from calligraphy. Rather it is meant to create form, not the goal of that form. The statement becomes an expression of the dynamic forward thinking group called Optimists. It denies the ossification of a simple heraldic identification and speaks of the spirited action of men gathered in fellowship.

"How you, the individual Optimist, relates to this symbol can only be determined by you in times to come. Just please do not be trapped in a 'like' or 'dislike' syndrome. That you are free to do—if you also accept the challenge to make your organization and your personal involvement grow and take meaningful action in the world."

There it stands today before the Optimist International office building on a busy thoroughfare in St. Louis, at once a symbol, a challenge and an inspiration to all Optimists who come to visit or on Optimist business. To the many thousands who pass daily, the sculpture and the handsome building provide impressive evidence that their world is just a little better because of men who call themselves Optimists.

CHAPTER 14

THE PASSING OF EACH YEAR
finds new faces in the over-all Optimist picture, from the club
level through the districts, up to the functioning of Optimist
International.

International presidents, vice-presidents and committee members in turn devote their time, energies and abilities to the advancement of Optimist International and, having served their
terms, vacate their posts that others may meet the challenges and
shoulder the responsibilities.

In many respects, the key man in the continuity of Optimist
International is its executive secretary. Since its inception the organization has been blessed in this respect with men of exceptional calibre.

His is a career that calls for the wearing of many different
hats. He sits with the Board of Directors and is charged with the
responsibility of interpreting its policies and administering its
directives. He is the organization's executive managing officer.

He is editor of The Optimist Magazine. He coordinates and supervises each of the several departments within the International office and, supervises both budgeting and expenditures.

In its infant years Optimist International had no headquarters nor professional secretary. Records, minutes and other vital documents were kept in a single drawer of the secretary's filing cabinet and sometimes carried about in his briefcase or jacket pocket.

During the period of 1919-22, Harry G. Hill of Indianapolis served as voluntary secretary. He was followed by another unpaid but devoted Optimist, Victor O. Post of San Francisco, who served for a few months but was neither an officer nor a member of the Executive Committee. First paid professional was Thomas B. Elliott of St. Louis who served as secretary-treasurer for five years, from 1923 to 1928.

At the 1929 Optimist International convention in Tulsa delegates heard their first report from Russell F. Meyer of St. Louis who was to serve as the key man for a quarter of a century.

Both the official records and the memories of long time Optimists indicate clearly that Russell F. Meyer, during his 25-year tenure laid the foundation stones for the solid and steady growth Optimist International has enjoyed and will continue to enjoy for many years to come.

The May, 1954, edition of The Optimist Magazine announced to 45,000 Optimists in more than 950 clubs that their international organization had a new executive secretary. His name was Bernard B. Burford.

Twelve years later, in the August, 1966, issue, some 87,000 Optimists in 2400 clubs read in stunned disbelief that "Burf" was dead. He had died suddenly at his desk in the International Office on Wednesday afternoon, July 13, 1966.

A native of Colchester, Ill., he was a graduate of Knox College in Galesburg, Ill., and the National Institute of Chamber of Commerce Administration at Northwestern University. During the early years of his career, Burf served actively and effectively in leadership roles of the Junior Chamber of Commerce of Peoria and the State of Illinois. Following his terms as president of each, he served as a national director of the U. S. Jaycees.

Burf's abilities and enthusiasm for public service brought him nationwide recognition. As a Jaycee he received the R. N. Ingleson award as outstanding state president and the Illinois Key Man Award. In 1962 he was granted the title of Chartered Association Executive by the American Society of Association Executives for his consistently demonstrated high standards of service and professional achievements. From 1963 until his death he was chairman of the U. S. Savings Bonds National Organization Committee.

In 1965 Knox College singled Burf out for its Alumni Achievement Award for exceptional leadership and noteworthy contributions to the public betterment as chief executive of an international service organization.

From far and wide came memorial gifts, testifying to the esteem and affection in which Burf was held. These gifts were used to establish the Bernard B. Burford Memorial Fund at Knox College, to be applied toward a campus project.

President Bob Leonard was at the International Office arranging his travels for his year, when Burf died. Immediately he appointed a special committee of past presidents to recommend to the Board a successor to the late executive secretary.

Dozens of applicants were screened and interviewed, backgrounds and qualifications were studied carefully and considered thoughtfully before the decision was made.

The January, 1967, Optimist Magazine brought the news that the Board of Directors had reached into the ranks of its fellow volunteers to find the man to take the helm as Executive Secretary.

Since the first of that month the position had been filled by Hugh H. Cranford of Charlotte, N. C., a man with 19 years of service to the organization at club, district and International levels. At 46 he had behind him a record of outstanding leadership as president of the Optimist Club of Charlotte, governor of District 18 (North and South Carolina), director of Optimist International and seven years of dedicated and effective service as chairman of three International committees.

As with his predecessor, Hugh began making his mark in the field of service to others early in his career. In 1953 he was presented the Young Man of the Year Award by the Charlotte Jaycees, recognizing his contributions to society through Sales and Marketing Executives International, Travelers Aid Society,

United Cerebral Palsy organization, the Boy Scouts, the Governor's Traffic Safety Council of North Carolina, the Masons, the Shrine and the Presbyterian Church where he had taught a class of adults for ten years.

During his remarks at the 1967 convention in Portland, Ore., his first as a professional Optimist, Hugh told the assembly that though he had attended many International conventions in one sense he felt that this was his first because "I find myself wearing an entirely different hat."

He continued, "I do not feel alone; I do not feel uncomfortable, but like my predecessors in this situation I feel the responsibility and the challenge. I accept both.

"The task of administrative management is an awesome one today for the history of Optimist International, like the history of our civilization, is a story of continuous change.

"It was only 17 years ago that we had no such thing as national TV programming, no computers, no satellites or other hardware orbiting the earth. That's less time than I have spent in fellowship in this organization, which gives you some idea of the change that takes place all around us in our society today."

Year by year the changes continue. Each sees a new Optimist administration, dedicated to keeping faith with fundamentals while at the same time keeping pace with a changing world.

Delegates to the 1966 convention in Baltimore elected Robert H. Leonard president; in 1967 in Portland, William R. Newhouse; in 1968 in Louisville, Gene Sternberg; in 1969 at Bal Harbour, Fla., Monroe Marlowe; at Los Angeles in 1970, Charles C. Campbell; at Minneapolis in 1971, Norman Shipley; at Montreal in 1972, S. Phil McCardwell. President-elect and ready to take over the reins for the 1973/74 year Ronald E. Thompson.

Though new leadership comes each Optimist year there is no real break in continuity. Programs and projects are often years in the making. There are no crash programs or snap decisions at the International level; every proposed change is weighed carefully and tested well by successive groups for there is a lot of machinery in the inner workshops of Optimist International and none of it is designed to be used on unwise or frivolous innovations.

As the Optimist organization continued to expand over the

Northern Hemisphere so did the scope of its service continue to widen. Fittingly, the reorganization and expansion of the professional staff at the International office in St. Louis has kept the pace through the years to better serve Optimists of the United States and Canada.

Not since 1937 has Optimist International been served by a secretary-treasurer alone. A few major upgrading changes along the way:

The assistant secretary appointed in 1937 became managing editor of The Optimist Magazine in 1942. Two years later the post of extension director, now new club director, was created. A boys work secretary, named in 1946, became boys work director in 1950. In 1972 both the director and the International Boys Work Committee broadened their field and became youth activities director and committee.

In 1953 the managing editor became public relations director; in 1964 The Optimist Magazine was removed from Public Relations Department to become a separate function. The public relations director, in 1966, became publicity director. Along the way the staff was increased to include a club service director, accounting and personnel director, supplies and purchasing director, administrative assistant and associate executive secretary.

Some other expansions and innovations—

Community Service Committee established as an International rotating committee in 1963; Community Service Department created in October, 1964.

New Club Services Department established in 1969 to establish regular communication with clubs two years old or less. The following year it was absorbed into the Club Services Department.

Leadership Training Committee, now Leadership Development Committee, established in 1967 to research, develop and maintain a sound training program for club and district officers and chairmen. To further the program, a Leadership Development Department was added in 1970.

Though the Community Service Committee remained unchanged, the Community Service Department in 1969 became the Activities Department.

As our society continues to change so are there opening new

133

avenues of need that may be met best by service clubs such as Optimist International through activities of its many clubs and members. To guide and assist them in their programs there must be a well-organized and completely competent staff of dedicated professionals.

The willingness to change with the times, to meet each demand as it arises, and the achievements of Optimist clubs everywhere may be traced to the devotion, the mobility and the competence of both professionals and volunteers.

Harry G. Hill
1919-1922

Harry B. Lewis
1922-1923

Thomas B. Elliott
1923-1928

Russell F. Meyer
1928-1953

Bernard B. Burford
1954-1966

Hugh H. Cranford
1967-

CHAPTER 15

In JUNE OF 1962
the Optimist International convention was held in St. Louis for a
very particular reason.

The Optimists had come for the dedication of their handsome
new International Office building. For years the staff had been
operating from offices in the Railway Exchange Building, an an-
cient structure in the St. Louis downtown area. As the organization grew the offices were expanded. Unfortunately the building
housed other tenants as well and it was not possible always to
secure adjoining or even abutting rooms. As a consequence the
several Optimist offices were widely scattered throughout the
building, making for a most inefficient operation.

But now they had an entire building all their own.

At the time there were more than 75,000 Optimists belonging
to 2,053 clubs.

Both members and the professional staff were proud of their
spacious new headquarters and were confident it would provide

ample room for 25 or 30 years.

Perhaps that's why they are called Optimists!

Seven years later, at the convention at Miami Beach, delegates voted to re-activate their building fund and assess each member fifty cents a year for the purpose.

In 1974 the building committee began in earnest to look positively at future needs. It was obvious even then that the rapidly growing organization would need more room for its headquarters and the necessarily larger staff.

Every possibility was explored thoroughly. The idea of selling the present building and constructing a new and larger one in another location was given thoughtful consideration. Proposed sites were visited. Existing structures up for sale were inspected.

Past International President William R. Newhouse of Madison, Wis., was chairman of the building committee. Serving with him after 1974 were Past President Dr. Carl L. Bowen of Albemarle, N. C., Terrence M. Cassaday of Burlington, Ontario, W. Arnold Chambers of Chattanooga, Tenn., and Executive Secretary Hugh H. Cranford of St. Louis.

Men who had served earlier on the project included Richard S. McAnany of Shawnee, Kan., (International President in 1976/77), Past President Gene H. Sternberg of Granite City, Ill., and Malcolm McDonald of Oakville, Ontario.

After months of deliberation the committee came forth with a definite proposal which was adopted with enthusiasm by the organization.

A new three-story tower, adjacent to and connected to the present office building would be built on the lot used for staff and visitors' parking.

As designed, the addition would add approximately 15,000 more square feet of office space plus an underground parking garage.

Target date for completion of the new building was Fall 1978.

This time the Optimists were being a little more realistic with their long range planning. They had seen their organization grow from 75,000 to more than 122,000 members, from 2053 to over 3400 clubs, in just 15 years and were confident the growth would continue.

The new building was designed not only in a style to comple-

Artist's rendition of the three-story addition to the International Office

ment the modern-style original building but sturdy enough to support two more stories when they are needed.

And needed one day in the future they will be, of that the men are sure. Could *that* be the reason they are called Optimists?

No longer would visitors find three people working in an office designed for one. And no longer find the supply room packed to the ceiling with cartons, boxes and files of materials needed to fill every Optimist club's needs.

As with every operation conducted by human beings, the faces seen at Optimist headquarters are changing with the passing years.

Gone from the current scene are those who for so many years were familiar to so many. They served the organization with an unflagging loyalty and with consummate skill and were well deserving of retirement with dignity. Ray Millard moved from St. Louis to the Houston, Tex., area. Remaining in St. Louis were John Parker, Bill Bailey, Larry Payne and Lou Jurinich.

Some of the new faces to be found at headquarters belong to Paul Houghland, Jr., Activities Director; Jim Carr, Publicity Director; V. A. "Ben" Bradshaw, Purchasing and Supply Director; David Blum, Convention Manager; Bud Floor, Youth Activities Director; Larry Walton, Leadership Development Director and Jerry Soke, manager of the data processing department.

Gary Adamson, in 1976 in addition to being editor of The Optimist Magazine, was given the responsibility of the new graphics department, and Ralph Gentles in 1977 was named associate executive secretary.

At each international convention the delegates vote for outstanding Optimists to lead their organization for the coming months.

Officers elected at the international convention include a president-elect and eight vice-presidents who, with the president, who automatically becomes president-designate at the convention, the executive secretary, and the two most immediate past presidents make up the board of directors.

At the 1972 convention delegates elected Ronald E. Thompson, a lawyer in Tacoma, Wash., as president-elect and on October 1, 1973 he took office as President; Ralph Glasscock, a business executive in Clinton, Mo., became President on October 1, 1974; in 1975 it was Patrick L. Grady, a road surfacing contractor from Indianapolis, Ind.; Richard S. McAnany, an asphalt contractor in Shawnee, Kan., served in 1976/77; Don L. Arnwine, a hospital administrator from Charleston, West Virginia, assumed the presidency in 1977; and Dudley D. Williams, elected president-elect in July, 1977, will take over the reins on October 1, 1978.

Meanwhile, the passing years have taken their toll of some of the men who through their devotion and energy built so well the foundation stones upon which today's organization is built.

Death has taken from our ranks several Optimists who served as President, some in our early years, others in more recent administrations. In the year 1969 two of the early Presidents passed away, Robert J. Sutherland, President in 1930/31, and Dr. F. Fern Petty, 1938/39 President. Franklin A. Steinko, President in 1949/50 died in 1970; 1941/42 and 1942/43 Presidents Eldon S. Dummitt and R. Carter Tucker, were taken in 1973. Harlington Wood, President in 1928/29, died in 1974, and George O. Browne and Walter J. Pray, both from Indianapolis, died in 1975. C. Ed Hall, 1927/28 President, passed away in 1976, and in the year 1977 we lost three Presidents and Optimist International's general counsel. The Presidents were Ralph Glasscock, 1974/75; Oscar A. Smith, 1926/27; and Norman L. Shipley, 1971/72; Wilburn A. Duncan served as OI's general counsel from 1959 until his death early in 1977.

CHAPTER 16

AS THE YEARS ROLL ON
the organization as well as the spirit of Optimism spreads in ever
widening circles.

The administrative year of 1976-77 saw the chartering of the
Optimist Club of Lewiston in Maine, a state which had been void
of Optimist clubs for several years. A few years prior the Optimist
Club of Anchorage, Alaska, was organized.

Because of the future possibilities for growth in these two areas,
International officials participated in the charter presentations
of these new clubs. President Ralph Glasscock and Executive
Secretary Hugh Cranford attended the charter banquet of the
Anchorage club in early 1975 and President Richard S. McAnany
presented the charter to the Optimist Club of Lewiston in 1977.
Shortly before the Lewiston event, the organization was shocked
to learn of the untimely death of Past President Ralph Glasscock.
According to the Bylaws of Optimist International his place on
the Board of Directors was filled by Past President Ronald E.

Thompson who had preceded him in office.

Just as there have been progressive changes in Optimism and its programs, in its staff and property, so has there been a change in its "image."

As we read in an earlier chapter, our first emblem, or logo, was a cartoon-like picture of a moon-faced man with a big grin on his face. There have been other advancements along this line, too. And 1977 saw the most recent, a sophisticated new emblem.

Investigation into a new, modern design that would reflect the tone of the 1970's and 1980's had begun many years before, and the letters O and I in a free-standing form was developed from the first concept of a new design. This was further refined and the initials were incorporated within the traditional octagon.

The emblem was copyrighted when President McAnany gave it official sanction and approved its use in the logotype for his slogan for the year, "Committed to Excellence." The new emblem went into use on several publications, stationery and other printed materials.

It has been offered to clubs and districts along with the traditional "Rising Sun" emblem that has been in use in slightly varying forms since 1923.

Though many clubs and districts adopted the new emblem immediately, the change-over in all probability will take several years. Older clubs will cherish their original banners forever. Older members will continue to wear the traditional pins. In the meantime, there will be nothing wrong or in bad taste about this as both emblems may be used interchangeably in good order.

During the year 1976, however, Optimists everywhere and Optimism on all levels were concentrating on an even greater emblem, The Great Seal of the United States of America. It was America's 200th anniversary—its Bicentennial—and they were not about to let it pass without paying proper and enthusiastic tribute.

International President Patrick L. Grady made available to one outstanding Optimist in each club the International President's Award, a beautifully designed pen holder for the Optimist's desk, in a style in keeping with the Bicentennial. Each club was invited to select and submit the name of the recipient.

Optimist International commissioned a talented artist, Biven,

to create a unique artpiece, a 20″ by 25″ montage, and made it available to clubs to provide them with a Bicentennial contribution to their communities. It was a handsome work of art, framed, and suitable for display in any public building. Individual Optimists could purchase them, too, for their homes or offices.

The montage was beautifully done and reproduced in limited number on manmade marble. Each one was numbered. The first was presented to President Gerald Ford, an Optimist from Grand Rapids. Number Two went to the Smithsonian Institution.

The skillfully executed artpiece depicted events and personalities down through American history with specific attention paid to the milestones of Optimist International that were interwoven into the theme.

Although the Optimists took time out to demonstrate their patriotism, they did not slacken their services to their home communities.

As you may recall, the first motto of Optimism was "Friend of the Delinquent Boy." The word "Delinquent" was wisely dropped after a year or two.

As Optimists expanded their programs to include girls the motto was altered again, this time to "Friend of Youth."

It might be more accurate to call the organization "Friend of Just About Everybody" as in addition to continuing its youth programs as described in earlier chapters and adding even more, the Optimists have spread their services to citizens of all walks of life and of all ages. The Tri-Star athletic program for boys and girls has been expanded to include golf and hockey as well as basketball.

In 1974, after several discussions with H.U.D. officials, Optimist International launched a new program called "Adopt A Neighborhood."

The program recommends that a metropolitan club select a definable small area in an inner-city neighborhood, such as a public housing development. A youth center, church or school may be used as a focal point. While the main objective of the Optimist volunteers would be to provide service, guidance and help to disadvantaged youth, they would also serve the entire community in many ways.

One of the first and most exciting Adopt A Neighborhood reports came from the Optimist Club of Eastside San Antonio, chartered in January, 1973, with 117 members.

With Hubert Lovelady, president, setting the pace the new Optimists took off like a moon-bound Apollo. They selected Sutton Homes, a public housing development, both because it was a neighborhood in need and because of a pledge of cooperation from local housing authorities.

First project was obvious—clean up the place.

The Optimists turned out en masse and were joined by both kids and adults in the area in a massive one-day clean-up. Truckloads of trash and litter were hauled away. Residents of Sutton Homes took new pride in their neighborhood and there have been no complaints of littering there since. They recognized the Optimists as more than just friends. They were benefactors.

After this demonstration both old and young were quick and eager to cooperate, to assist and take an active part in any project the Optimists would tackle.

They staged a kite flying contest for 150 youngsters. They bought a supply of window glass and helped residents replace broken panes. Fifteen hundred young people attended the Optimists' Career Conference Day. They set up a Youth Summer Employment Program. They funded 13 camperships for Girl Scouts. Residents of the neighborhood were so impressed they went out and raised money to send 310 more.

And the work continued, Optimists and residents working hand in hand on one project after another.

Are the Optimists rewarded for their effort? Are the residents appreciative? All they have to do is remember what Sutton Homes was like before their friends, the Optimists, "adopted" them.

In the International Office city the Optimist Club of St. Louis performed a similar service in the Murphy-Blair community.

Here the activity was centered around a facility where old and young alike can go to improve their educational and cultural levels. Among other services provided are 100 meals five days a week.

Throughout the school year the center provides weekly and monthly programs from tutoring and physical fitness to black culture and games in the game room.

In all, $94,600 a year is spent on and in the center.

How does a club of 79 members raise that kind of money? It doesn't. But it does come in with a little over $1000 a year.

This is only "seed money" for the thousands more provided by federal and local governments, United Way, and others.

But it took the Optimists to get the great program off the ground!

Optimists' new community service projects cover a wide spectrum of programs. Some are co-ordinated on an international basis by committees working at headquarters. But most of them are seen and acted upon at the local level as the needs of communities vary widely.

For one example, in the Spiritual and Religious field, let's take a quick look at what the Breakfast Optimist Club of Columbia, S. C., did in early December of 1976.

At the request of the Governor of South Carolina, the 56-member club organized and staged a "Carolighting" service to bring in the Christmas season.

They began work in August in an "all hands on deck" operation.

Then, on December 5, it all came to a head. On the statehouse grounds there assembled an all-star band of 500 select teenagers from schools all over the state, ten handbell choirs from South Carolina churches, a mass choir of 1600 voices from churches and schools, the University of South Carolina's award winning concert choir and a special children's choir of 4th, 5th and 6th graders.

The relatively small Optimist club was the sole sponsor of this meaningful and spectacular ushering in of the Yuletide season.

There were but 27 members in the Optimist Club of Merriam, Kan., but they tackled a unique operation in the area of safety.

Working with the police, fire and other departments of their city they conducted a seminar for baby sitters. On two successive Saturdays highly trained professionals gave talks and demonstrations in the areas of handling emergencies, infant care, mouth-to-mouth resuscitation, interviewing parents for essential information and the like.

Each certified baby sitter was given an emergency phone number for use 24 hours a day, seven days a week. The phone is at the Merriam fire station with well qualified firemen on hand to answer questions, give advice or send help.

Thanks to the Optimists young Merriam parents leave their children in competent hands and enjoy their hours away from home with greater peace of mind. And the entire community is well aware of who brought it all about!

The Optimist Club of Forest Glade in Windsor, Ontario, was another small club that pulled off a great project.

In the area of International Relationships they staged a three-day International Floor Hockey Tournament.

Invited to participate were teams from Battle Creek and Buchanan, Mich. They stayed in private homes, learned more of each other, played and ate together and returned to their homes with many new, good friends.

But first it was necessary to organize their own league to participate. This was done at the local community center with the aid of the Parks and Recreation people of the city.

When completed the league consisted of 144 boys and girls involved in and enjoying an on-going program. Their plan was to meet again in 1978 in Battle Creek.

Meanwhile, in the sunny South, the 65 members of the Optimist Club of North Pensacola in Florida worked for a solid year on their project in the area of Community Improvement. And at the end of that successful year they had completed only Phase 1 and the work continued.

For 15 years the city had owned a 16-acre plot in the heart of the residential area. Annually, the city fathers would search their coffers for money to create there a beautiful park for both young and old. They always came up empty handed.

Then the Optimists took over.

Starting with $9000 of their own money they set out to raise $100,000 for the recreational area.

Of course there was no way they could do it alone but they got the ball rolling and they got plenty of help from both citizens groups and government agencies.

The Optimists did most of the construction work themselves.

At the end of their first year the Optimists, with the help of others, had purchased playground equipment, had a one-mile paved parking lot, fencing, picnic tables, two ballfields with backstops and a concession stand foundation. They also had completed their drainage and water systems.

It was the largest single project ever taken on by a service club in that area.

Pensacolans are today and will be for years to come proud of their improving Hitzman-Optimist Park.

As has been mentioned, the ways in which Optimists serve their home communities are most diversified.

One of the most rewarding and worthwhile programs was conducted by the 86-member Optimist Club of Kent in Grand Rapids, Mich., in the area of Health and Welfare.

They sponsored a special Olympics tourney for more than 900 mentally retarded, and otherwise handicapped youngsters of Kent County and Grand Rapids.

Theirs was a $45,000 project and it provided the opportunity for the children to compete in athletic events, share the experiences of athletic competition and find joy and excitement that they otherwise would be denied.

This is the most rewarding endeavor that any service club could conduct for its community and it was an overwhelming success for the Kent Optimists and the citizens of the entire county of Kent, the chairman appraised the effort at its conclusion.

And there are many, Optimists and non-Optimists alike, who are inclined to agree.

CHAPTER 17

O N DECEMBER 19, 1776, The Pennsylvania Journal published an article, "The American Crisis," that had been submitted by a citizen named Thomas Paine. In it he expressed, in a simple, eight-word sentence, the complicated and constantly worrisome thought that was uppermost in the minds of all thinking people of his day:

"These are the times that try men's souls."

And indeed they were for already underway was what turned out to be a long and bitter struggle to gain independence from England and to establish on this continent a new nation, based on the then almost universally considered ridiculous idea that a government should serve its people rather than the people serve their government.

In Paine's opinion, the greater the sacrifice and the more bitter the conflict the more cherished would be the ultimate triumph. As he put it,

"What we obtain too cheap, we esteem too lightly; it is dearness only that gives everything its value."

Though he was writing then of a current grave situation, what he had to say has been applicable to every succeeding generation and era on the North American Continent and, most certainly, are truths that serve—or should be serving—as brilliant guidelights for men more than casually concerned about society today, and of even greater importance, that of tomorrow.

For many years the most pressing problems were those confronting the family, the neighborhood and the individual community. Men of good will and action met them head-on and fought them to the best of their ability, usually with some degree of success.

Following World War Two, however, there was an incredible speed-up of communication, transportation and industrial expansion. These brought to almost every city, town and hamlet, however remote, many advantages. Along with these, unfortunately, came some serious problems that were new to most communities.

What had been prevalent in relatively few isolated places in the United States and Canada now began to threaten the lives of everyone everywhere.

Before many were aware of it we were drifting toward the chaos that can result only from the disintegration into a permissive society. As has been said so wisely, "If the Lord had intended ours to be a permissive society, He would have given Moses ten suggestions."

Again, it became the challenge and responsibility of all Optimists to combat these problems in a new and effective way. To do this it was necessary to devise programs and plans that would apply to the efforts of Optimist clubs that would enable them while working at the local level to add materially to the improvement of the International picture.

Of equal importance were the increasing needs to keep updating time honored labors in the fields of youth and community service at the local level.

Since its founding Optimist International had been funded solely by dues paid by Optimists. For a time this was sufficient. In recent years, however, it became more and more obvious that this was placing a limit on the service to clubs, especially when it came to enlarging and broadening the scope of existing activities and the creation of sorely needed new ones.

Such increased services could be supplied only after the expenditure of three vital resources, Time, Work and Money.

Out of this situation came the newest and perhaps most exciting program—The Optimist International Foundation. Like all far reaching and long lasting programs, it was not born overnight. It emerged in its completed form only after countless hours of study, research and serious reflection.

Having arrived at a decision on the fundamental needs for and goals of the program, the Board of Directors in 1969 instructed Optimist International's Finance Committee to go to work on the detailed creation of the proposed Foundation.

Again, this was not a project that could be carried out at a single session. Every stone that went into the structure had to be, and was, examined thoroughly, tested carefully and measured for accuracy. More hours, more talents and more devoted energy were applied until at last the committee was prepared to report its recommendations for the launching of the Optimist International Foundation.

At the 1971 convention in Minneapolis Past International President Sternberg announced to delegates that their new Foundation had been approved by the Board, that all necessary legal steps had been taken and that it was in business.

He outlined the general purpose of the Foundation: "This corporation is created and shall be operated exclusively for the charitable, literary and educational purposes and activities of Optimist International."

The initial fund-raising goal of the Foundation is neither an overly modest nor overly ambitious one. It was arrived at as the proper amount to expand current Optimist programs and to meet effectively new challenges and opportunities for service that are rising at an ever quickening pace.

The original goal is fixed at one million dollars.

As the Foundation is a not-for-profit, U. S. tax exempt corporation, its creators are confident the goal will be reached through contributions and gifts from Optimists and others who have found or will find that this service organization's methods of meeting head-on the problems of today can lead only to a

150

better tomorrow.

Monroe Marlowe, past International president and one of the original board members of the Foundation, outlined the basic needs and functions of the new program in an article he wrote for The Optimist Magazine:

"We must constantly be aware of what is taking place in the world and recognize important changes, drastic upheavals of tradition and custom, yet always be willing and able to change. We must also realize that only by adapting our activities to those changes can we continue to grow and develop.

"In Optimist International we have long known that many of the activities we have conducted for so many years no longer meet the needs of all members and their communities. . . . . But development of new programs, new concepts and new ideas is expensive. It takes time and money to experiment, to test and to evaluate.

"The Foundation will facilitate an increase in program research and the development of new and additional programs with which Optimist International, its clubs and members may meet and serve the challenges and needs of our changing society. Through the resources of the Foundation, programs of Optimist International can attain nation-wide exposure in the United States and Canada to gain and influence public support and participation."

It has been observed by professional viewers of our times that many of the major problems that confront us are inter-related—crime in the streets, burglaries, drug abuse, spread of venereal diseases, juvenile delinquents and runaways, pornography and obscene movies.

Could these evils have grown to such proportions in a well disciplined, self respecting society living in a land where streams flowed unpolluted, the air was pure, trash and waste materials disposed of sensibly and the beauty and blessings of Nature carefully preserved?

It is small wonder, then, that an opinion poll revealed that, at long last, people have become aware of the size of the main problem that has grown about them and that they now regard pollution as the most serious social enemy that confronts them. The poll also revealed they shared an interesting and, to them, a perplexing question, "But what can I as an individual or member of an organization do about it?"

For an answer to that, let us turn again to Foundation Director Marlowe:

"The board of the Foundation has pledged that the very first money which comes in will be used to research and explore for viable solutions to these problems (of our environment). We estimate that about $35,000 to $50,000 must be spent to develop one program which can effectively be used in all, or nearly all, of the communities represented by our more than 3,000 Optimist clubs.

"In other words, for about $15 per club, we can put into your hands the materials, the agenda and the know-how to develop a community-wide effort aimed at improving the environment in which you live and raise your children. . . .

"What I'm trying to say to you is this: We have at hand in the Foundation an opportunity to develop new programs and skills that can make our Optimist clubs the greatest force for community service, environmental protection, youth work and other worthwhile goals that we have ever seen."

Almost immediately following the first public announcement of the Foundation's creation and explanation of its immediate and long-range plans, the million-dollar campaign to fund its operations was off and running. Individual Optimists and Optimist clubs were, quite understandably, among the first to respond. It is anticipated, however, that as the program gets underway and the public begins to see what a beneficial impact it will have on communities contributions will come from other sources—other individuals, organizations, corporations and even governmental units, all of whom wish to demonstrate their faith and their confidence in the greatness of the Optimist International Foundation.

This, then, is perhaps the most ambitious forward giant stride taken by Optimist International since that day in 1919 in Louisville, when representatives of 11 Optimist clubs totalling 1298 members met to weld themselves into a unified body. Growth has been steady and strong as those good men brought together other good men under the banner of Optimist International.

At the time of its 50th convention in 1968 Optimist International knew of 16 men still living who had attended that first one. Each received a special invitation to return to Louisville and receive recognition for his early contributions to what was then a small, but is now a great and farflung, service organization.

And what is the reason for the strong and steady growth of the organization? It must go beyond the idea that in a given community, men of stature from business, industry and the professions merely enjoy a weekly meeting with friends and a stimulating program. It just cannot be that new Optimist clubs are organized by persuasive, volunteer "salesmen" simply so their own clubs may register high on the Achievements and Awards list.

No, there can be but one fundamental reason—The philosophy and workings of the organization and its ability to keep the pace during changing times, provide the answers to what every man in every community needs!

One of the finest definitions of this philosophy was given by International President C. Edd Hall in his keynote address at the tenth annual convention in 1928:

"The kingdom of the Corsican decayed with the passing years, but the Empire of the Nazarene grows greater day by day. His philosophy was the philosophy of sacrifice and service. His goal was the unseen shores to which mankind may aspire. His dream was that all people of every age, land or clime should arise to the destiny which God and Nature have decreed they might assume.

Optimist International, not being a small thing, has found ample room in society for growth. There is no reason to believe that the end of that growth is yet in sight. With the stimulus provided by the Optimist International Foundation and its far reaching new programs, the name and fame of the organization and its work will spread even more rapidly. With an eye toward O.I.'s brighter than ever potential, it is interesting to note how some of its still active former leaders foresee the future of our organization.

W H. (Bill) Pierce of Dallas, International President, 1946-47: "I believe that Optimists will occupy themselves more with governmental and world affairs than they do at the moment. . . . We cannot have a world of peace unless there is an end to the competition for the necessities of life. Politicians, regardless of their sincerity, cannot accomplish this nor bridge the gap but service clubs such as Optimist International can, merely by following their aims and objectives as they are already accepted and by carrying them to the rest of the world. This is a large order but nothing less can justify our continued existence."

Dr. Carl L. Bowen of Albemarle, N. C., International President, 1964-65: "Optimism is on the threshold of its finest hour. More important than increased membership will be our scope of service to mankind. We will see an expanded program of work to include all areas of community and national service. A greater membership, an expanded program of service, an organization changing to meet the needs of a changing world will put Optimist International in the forefront in stature, in influence and in service by the year 2000."

John W. Whatley of Atlanta, Ga., International President, 1960-61: "I believe that Optimist International has now reached a level of maturity that will give us a steady growth across the foreseeable future without the lunges in various directions that we had had in the past. I like the looks of what I see ahead for it is something that we have worked for a long time and I think we are pulling nearer the ideal organization than we have ever been before."

Dr. Walter A. Reiling of Dayton, Ohio, International President, 1953-54: "I predict that Optimist International by the year 2000 will be four times larger than at present. Community service will become a program equal to and probably exceeding boys work, which will very likely be known as youth work. Community service probably will be involved in outlining, securing and creating recreational facilities for people of all ages, but particularly for middle-aged and older citizens. The need for adequate recreational outlets will be one of the most pressing needs during the next 25 years."

Dr. George Cobley of Santa Monica, Calif., International President, 1963-64: "I foresee a brighter day tomorrow, not only for O.I. but for the entire society of the free world. I see a swing from government encroachment in the fields of community welfare and service, back to individual responsibility as our people wake up to the fact that they can do it better for themselves than others can do it for them. Men have always found it easier to work in groups than by themselves, and thus service clubs offer a natural force in which to participate.

"We do not hestiate to take bold steps forward if it is to be for our betterment. In this we take great pride and enjoy great confidence. This spirit will continue in our leadership. We are stepping up from a first class organization to a deluxe organization. The prestige of Optimist International and many of the members will expand greatly as our leadership continues to develop and individual initiative again becomes stylish."

Ask any officer of Optimist International, past or current; ask any past or present leader at the district or club level; ask any good Optimist anywhere and you will receive replies similar to those cited here.

Those who know, who live it and work at it, see ahead for it greater achievements, greater service, greater stature. Why? Because Optimists believe there is no other philosophy quite like ours. They know it is the easiest to understand and adopt, the least difficult to demonstrate and explain, the most serviceable to the widest range of personalities and skills.

They have found out for themselves that a man can face anything life has to offer, with calm confidence. He steadfastly believes with the poet that—

"It matters not how strait the gate,
How charged with punishment the scroll;
I am the master of my fate,
I am the captain of my soul!"

Optimists have seen that their philosophy does not conflict with any creed or religion but, rather, enhances the values of them all.

The record is both clear and emphatic. This organization does indeed motivate the best in social environment, for it is a shining and forceful positive in a world of negatives.

A few months before his untimely death, the author asked then Executive Secretary Bernard B. Burford for an expression of his personal thoughts on the organization and what he foresaw for it in the years that lay ahead.

How prophetic he was:

"To be born free was an accident, to live free is a responsibility, and to die free is an obligation. Our future lies in the hearts and minds of those who, through this organization, are dedicated to preserving this freedom for all and who believe that our ultimate destiny lies along the path of service to one's fellowman.

"So into the hands of those who follow we place a great heritage of the past and a present of magnificent achievements. May they be accepted with loving care and trust for they represent the hopes, the dreams and, yes, even the tears of a labor of love of those thousands of Optimists who have trod the noble path.

"On such a solid foundation, we know no limitation in the years that lie ahead."

APPENDIX A

Officers, Boards of Governors, Executive Committees and Boards of Directors of Optimist International

1919-1920

OFFICERS

President—William H. Harrison,
Louisville, Ky.
1st Vice President—Earl B. Bowman,
St. Louis, Mo.
2nd Vice President—E. L. Monser,
Buffalo, N. Y.
Secretary—Dr. Harry G. Hill,
Indianapolis, Ind.
Treasurer—William C. Snyder,
Kansas City, Mo.

BOARD OF GOVERNORS

William H. Harrison; Earl B. Bowman; E. L. Monser; William C. Snyder; C. E. DeLong, Syracuse, N. Y., Section 1; J. L. Schoen, Chicago, Ill., Appointed to represent Section 2; J. M. Schmid, Indianapolis, Ind., Section 3; Rupert F. Fry, Milwaukee, Wis., Section 4; C. Jasper Bell, Kansas City, Mo., Section 5; W. K. Robertson, Springfield, Ill., Section 6; C. Jasper Bell, Kansas City, Mo., Appointed to represent Section 7

1920-1921

OFFICERS

President—William H. Harrison,
Louisville, Ky.
1st Vice President—S. M. Henley,
Kansas City, Mo.
2nd Vice President—H. T. Watson,
Los Angeles, Calif.
3rd Vice President—Ernst F. Bethke,
Milwaukee, Wis.
4th Vice President—Dr. Martin Ritter,
Chicago, Ill.
Treasurer—Harry B. Lewis,
Springfield, Ill.

EXECUTIVE COMMITTEE

William H. Harrison; S. M. Henley; O. L. Prohaska, Governor,
Chicago, Ill.; James W. Chilton, Governor, St. Louis, Mo.; Dr. Harry
G. Hill, Secretary, Indianapolis, Ind.

1921-1922

OFFICERS

President—Cyrus Crane Willmore,
St. Louis, Mo.
1st Vice President—William B. Guyton,
Los Angeles, Calif.
2nd Vice President—J. Bailey Wray,
Knoxville, Tenn.
3rd Vice President—O. L. Prohaska,
Chicago, Ill.
4th Vice President—E. E. Fisher,
Columbus, Ohio
Treasurer—Harry B. Lewis,
Springfield, Ill.
Secretary—Dr. Harry G. Hill,
Indianapolis, Ind.

EXECUTIVE COMMITTEE

Cyrus Crane Willmore; J. Bailey Wray; Harry B. Lewis; Dr. Harry
G. Hill; Ernst F. Bethke, Governor, Milwaukee, Wis.; E. E. Hagler,
Governor, Springfield, Ill.; J. M. Schmid, Governor, Indianapolis,
Ind.

158

1922-1923

OFFICERS

President—Jack Martin,
  San Francisco, Calif.
1st Vice President—Frank O. Denney,
  Kansas City, Mo.
2nd Vice President—J. Bailey Wray,
  Knoxville, Tenn.
3rd Vice President—Walter Smith,
  St. Louis, Mo.
4th Vice President—Chester O. Fischer,
  Peoria, Ill.
Treasurer—Harry B. Lewis,
  Chicago, Ill. (Appointed secretary-
  treasurer in August, 1922)

EXECUTIVE COMMITTEE

Jack Martin; Chester O. Fischer; J. Bailey Wray; Harry B. Lewis;
Ernst F. Bethke, Governor, Milwaukee, Wis.; James W. Chilton,
Governor, St. Louis, Mo.; H. E. Garrett, Governor, Louisville, Ky.;
Victor O. Post, San Francisco, Calif., (Appointed secretary in June,
1922, but was not an officer nor on the executive committee)

1923-1924

OFFICERS

President—James W. Chilton,
  St. Louis, Mo.
1st Vice President—C. H. Converse,
  Oklahoma City, Okla.
2nd Vice President—George D. Welles,
  Toledo, Ohio
3rd Vice President—Harlington Wood,
  Springfield, Ill.
4th Vice President—Samuel R. Read,
  Chattanooga, Tenn.
Treasurer—Harry B. Lewis,
  Chicago, Ill.
Executive Secretary—Thomas B. Elliott,
  St. Louis, Mo. (Appointed June 16,
  1923)
Field Secretary—Jay C. Goodrich,
  St. Louis, Mo. (Appointed June 16,
  1923)

EXECUTIVE COMMITTEE

James W. Chilton; Harry B. Lewis; C. H. Converse; George D.
Welles; Harlington Wood; Dr. W. A. Hinckle, Governor, Peoria,
Ill.; E. H. Wenzel, Governor, Milwaukee, Wis.

1924-1925

OFFICERS

President—Sherman Rogers,
  New York, N. Y.
1st Vice President—Leo F. Nohl,
  Milwaukee, Wis.
2nd Vice President—Dr. Charles B.
  Kern, Lafayette, Ind.
3rd Vice President—H. O. Henderson,
  Long Beach, Calif.
4th Vice President—Roland A.
  McCrady, Pittsburgh, Pa.
Secretary-Treasurer—Thomas B. Elliott,
  St. Louis, Mo.

EXECUTIVE COMMITTEE

Sherman Rogers; Leo F. Nohl; Dr. Charles B. Kern; Thomas B.
Elliott; Harlington Wood, Governor, Springfield, Ill.; F. D. Zimmerman, Governor, Denver, Colo.; Nicholas F. Nolan, Governor, Dayton, Ohio

1925-1926

OFFICERS

President—Leo F. Nohl,
  Milwaukee, Wis.
1st Vice President—C. Edd Hall,
  Oklahoma City, Okla.
2nd Vice President—Hal Thurston,
  Kansas City, Mo.
3rd Vice President—Oscar A. Smith,
  Los Angeles, Calif.
4th Vice President—Nicholas F. Nolan,
  Dayton, Ohio
Secretary-Treasurer—Thomas B. Elliott,
  St. Louis, Mo.

EXECUTIVE COMMITTEE

Leo F. Nohl; C. Edd Hall; Hal Thurston; Nicholas F. Nolan;
Dr. Charles B. Kern, Governor, Lafayette, Ind.; Harlington Wood,
Governor, Springfield, Ill.

160

1926-1927

OFFICERS

President—Oscar A. Smith,
  Los Angeles, Calif.
1st Vice President—Nicholas F. Nolan,
  Dayton, Ohio
2nd Vice President—Paul W. Gibbons,
  Philadelphia, Pa.
3rd Vice President—A. B. Walker,
  Houston, Tex.
4th Vice President—E. Foster Chappell,
  Toronto, Ont.
Secretary-Treasurer—Thomas B. Elliott,
  St. Louis, Mo.

EXECUTIVE COMMITTEE

Oscar A. Smith; Leo F. Nohl, Immediate Past President (Honorary Member), Milwaukee, Wis.; Nicholas F. Nolan; Paul W. Gibbons; Holmes A. Sperb, Governor, San Francisco, Calif.; A. B. Chandler, Governor, Versailles, Ky.; Harlington Wood, Governor, Springfield, Ill.

1927-1928

OFFICERS

President—C. Edd Hall,
  Oklahoma City, Okla.
1st Vice President—Harlington Wood,
  Springfield, Ill.
2nd Vice President—Paul W. Gibbons,
  Philadelphia, Pa.
3rd Vice President—E. Foster Chappell,
  Toronto, Ont.
4th Vice President—Albert A. Adams,
  Chattanooga, Tenn.
Secretary-Treasurer—Thomas B. Elliott,
  St. Louis, Mo.

EXECUTIVE COMMITTEE

C. Edd Hall; Oscar A. Smith, Immediate Past President, (Honorary Member), Los Angeles, Calif.; Paul W. Gibbons; Harlington Wood; F. D. Zimmerman, Governor, Denver, Colo.; Dan W. Hayes, Governor, Lincoln, Neb., Appointed Jan. 1928, to replace F. D. Zimmerman, deceased; Bert King, Governor, Wichita Falls, Tex.; Willis B. Boyd, Governor, Johnson City, Tenn.

1928-1929

OFFICERS

President—Harlington Wood,
Springfield, Ill.
1st Vice President—Walter J. Pray,
Indianapolis, Ind.
2nd Vice President—Paul W. Gibbons,
Philadelphia, Pa.
3rd Vice President—Warren B. Bovard,
Los Angeles, Calif.
4th Vice President—Asbury Endicott,
Tulsa, Okla.
Secretary-Treasurer—Thomas B. Elliott,
St. Louis, Mo.
Secretary-Treasurer—Russell F. Meyer,
St. Louis, Mo. (Appointed Sept.
1928)

EXECUTIVE COMMITTEE

Harlington Wood; C. Edd Hall, Immediate Past President (Honorary
Member), Oklahoma City, Okla.; Walter J. Pray; Holmes A. Sperb,
Governor, San Francisco, Calif.; W. D. Paul Farthing, Governor,
East St. Louis, Ill.; Dan W. Hayes, Governor, Lincoln, Neb.; Bert
King, Governor, Wichita Falls, Tex.

1929-1930

OFFICERS

President—Nicholas F. Nolan,
Dayton, Ohio
Vice Presidents—
W. D. Paul Farthing,
East St. Louis, Ill.
Dan W. Hayes, Lincoln, Neb.
Warren B. Bovard,
Los Angeles, Calif.
Frank M. Peirce, Washington, D. C.
Secretary-Treasurer—Russell F. Meyer,
St. Louis, Mo.

EXECUTIVE COMMITTEE

Nicholas F. Nolan; Harlington Wood, Immediate Past President
(Honorary Member), Springfield, Ill.; W. D. Paul Farthing; Holmes
A. Sperb, Governor, San Francisco, Calif.; C. C. Atwell, Governor,
Columbus, Ohio; Kenneth A. Barker, Governor, Louisville, Ky.;
Harry D. Anderson, Governor, Syracuse, N. Y.; Walter J. Pray,
Governor (Honorary Member), Indianapolis, Ind.

162

1930-1931

OFFICERS

President—Robert J. Sutherland,
Madison, Wis.
Vice Presidents—
Kenneth A. Barker, Louisville, Ky.
Milton Schaffner, Erie, Pa.
Judge E. S. Matthias,
Columbus, Ohio
Holmes A. Sperb,
San Francisco, Calif.
Secretary-Treasurer—Russell F. Meyer,
St. Louis, Mo.

EXECUTIVE COMMITTEE

Robert J. Sutherland; Nicholas F. Nolan, Immediate Past President
(Honorary Member), Dayton, Ohio; Milton Schaffner; Holmes A.
Sperb; C. C. Atwell, Governor, Columbus, Ohio; Leon Jourolmon,
Governor, Knoxville, Tenn.; Damon E. Williams, Governor, Kansas
City, Mo.

1931-1932

OFFICERS

President—Holmes A. Sperb,
San Francisco, Calif.
Vice Presidents—
C. C. Atwell, Columbus, Ohio
Gordon B. Jackson, Toronto, Ont.
David W. Onan, Minneapolis, Minn.
Damon E. Williams,
Kansas City, Mo.
Secretary-Treasurer—Russell F. Meyer,
St. Louis, Mo.

EXECUTIVE COMMITTEE

Holmes A. Sperb; Robert J. Sutherland, Immediate Past President
(Honorary Member), Madison, Wis.; C. C. Atwell; David W. Onan;
Damon E. Williams; Dr. Seth P. Smith, Governor, St. Louis, Mo.;
Walter C. Wagner, Governor, Louisville, Ky.

1932-1933

OFFICERS

President—David W. Onan,
Minneapolis, Minn.
Vice Presidents—
Jeff Barnette, Houston, Tex.
Henry Schaffert, Washington, D. C.
Sam B. Ferris, Edmonton, Alta.
Maurice M. Walsh,
Birmingham, Ala.
Secretary-Treasurer—Russell F. Meyer,
St. Louis, Mo.

EXECUTIVE COMMITTEE

David W. Onan; Holmes A. Sperb, Immediate Past President, San Francisco, Calif.; Robert J. Sutherland, Past President, Madison, Wis.; V. Ernest Field, Governor, Indianapolis, Ind.; Merritt M. Ranstead, Governor, Chicago, Ill.; Walter C. Wagner, Governor, Louisville, Ky.; William R. Johnson, Governor, Denver, Colo.

1933-1934

OFFICERS

President—V. Ernest Field,
Indianapolis, Ind.
Vice Presidents—
James Booth, St. Petersburg, Fla.
George R. Dane, Toronto, Ont.
Theodore F. Peirce,
Los Angeles, Calif.
Walter C. Wagner, Louisville, Ky.
Secretary-Treasurer—Russell F. Meyer,
St. Louis, Mo.

EXECUTIVE COMMITTEE

V. Ernest Field; David W. Onan, Immediate Past President, Minneapolis, Minn.; Holmes A. Sperb, Past President, San Francisco, Calif.; Walter C. Wagner; Orrin L. Edwards, Governor, Minneapolis, Minn.; Will J. French, Governor, Topeka, Kan.; John G. Swope, Governor, San Antonio, Tex.

164

1934-1935

OFFICERS

President—Henry Schaffert,
  Washington, D. C.
Vice Presidents—
  J. C. Frederick, Detroit, Mich.
  Will J. French, Topeka, Kan.
  Dr. H. D. Pearson, Erie, Pa.
  Dr. F. Fern Petty,
    Los Angeles, Calif.
Secretary-Treasurer—Russell F. Meyer,
  St. Louis, Mo.

EXECUTIVE COMMITTEE

Henry Schaffert; V. Ernest Field, Immediate Past President, Indianapolis, Ind.; David W. Onan, Past President, Minneapolis, Minn.; John A. Henderson, Governor, Toronto, Ont.; Dr. Ralph H. Monger, Governor, Knoxville, Tenn.; Arthur C. Stock, Governor, Dayton, Ohio; John G. Swope, Governor, San Antonio, Tex.

1935-1936

OFFICERS

President—Walter J. Pray,
  Indianapolis, Ind.
Vice Presidents—
  Orrin L. Edwards,
    Minneapolis, Minn.
  Earl G. Stanza, St. Louis, Mo.
  John G. Swope, San Antonio, Tex.
  Walter C. Wagner, Louisville, Ky.
Secretary-Treasurer—Russell F. Meyer,
  St. Louis, Mo.

EXECUTIVE COMMITTEE

Walter J. Pray; Henry Schaffert, Immediate Past President, Washington, D. C.; V. Ernest Field, Past President, Indianapolis, Ind.; Orrin L. Edwards; Earl G. Stanza; Walter C. Wagner; Arthur C. Stock, Governor, Dayton, Ohio

1936-1937

OFFICERS

President—Earl G. Stanza,
St. Louis, Mo.
Vice Presidents—
Clarence H. McClean,
Kansas City, Mo.
Dr. Ralph H. Monger,
Knoxville, Tenn.
Donald M. Samson, Yakima, Wash.
William J. Tamblyn, Toronto, Ont.
Secretary-Treasurer—Russell F. Meyer,
St. Louis, Mo.

EXECUTIVE COMMITTEE

Earl G. Stanza; Walter J. Pray, Immediate Past President, Indianapolis, Ind.; Henry Schaffert, Past President, Washington, D. C.; Clarence H. McClean; Dr. Ralph H. Monger; William J. Tamblyn; Thomas F. O'Keefe, Governor, Detroit, Mich.

1937-1938

OFFICERS

President—William J. Tamblyn,
Toronto, Ont.
Vice Presidents—
Solon R. Featherston,
Wichita Falls, Tex.
Thomas F. O'Keefe, Detroit, Mich.
Ravee Norris, Richmond, Va.
Theodore F. Peirce,
Los Angeles, Calif.
Secretary-Treasurer—Russell F. Meyer,
St. Louis, Mo.

EXECUTIVE COMMITTEE

William J. Tamblyn; Earl G. Stanza, Immediate Past President, St. Louis, Mo.; Walter J. Pray, Past President, Indianapolis, Ind.; Solon R. Featherston; Ravee Norris; Thomas F. O'Keefe; Theodore F. Peirce

1938-1939

OFFICERS

President—Dr. F. Fern Petty,
Los Angeles, Calif.
Vice Presidents—
Emile O. Bloche, Oak Park, Ill.
Thomas F. O'Keefe, Detroit, Mich.
T. Howard Price, Towson, Md.
Frank A. Scharlott, St. Louis, Mo.
Secretary-Treasurer—Russell F. Meyer,
St. Louis, Mo.

EXECUTIVE COMMITTEE

Dr. F. Fern Petty; William J. Tamblyn, Immediate Past President,
Toronto, Ont.; Earl G. Stanza, Past President, St. Louis, Mo.;
Thomas F. O'Keefe; T. Howard Price; E. Tucker Carlton, Governor,
Richmond, Va.; John N. Free, Governor, Wichita, Kan.

1939-1940

OFFICERS

President—Thomas F. O'Keefe,
Detroit, Mich.
Vice Presidents—
Eldon S. Dummit, Lexington, Ky.
John N. Free, Wichita, Kan.
Leslie G. Pefferle, Springfield, Ill.
Robert C. Pepper, Ft. Worth, Tex.
Secretary-Treasurer—Russell F. Meyer,
St. Louis, Mo.

EXECUTIVE COMMITTEE

Thomas F. O'Keefe; Dr. F. Fern Petty, Immediate Past President,
Los Angeles, Calif.; William J. Tamblyn, Past President, Toronto,
Ont.; Eldon S. Dummit; John N. Free; Leslie G. Pefferle; Robert
C. Pepper

1940-1941

OFFICERS

President—John N. Free,
  Wichita, Kan.
Vice Presidents—
  Eldon S. Dummit, Lexington, Ky.
  Percy P. McCallum, Windsor, Ont.
  Lee A. Rose, Los Angeles, Calif.
  Harry P. Stuth, Corpus Christi, Tex.
Secretary-Treasurer—Russell F. Meyer,
  St. Louis, Mo.

EXECUTIVE COMMITTEE

John N. Free; Thomas F. O'Keefe, Immediate Past President, Detroit, Mich.; Dr. F. Fern Petty, Past President, Los Angeles, Calif.; Eldon S. Dummit; Harry P. Stuth; Earl Griffiths, Governor, Montclair, N. J.; Dr. Gordon H. Ira, Governor, Jacksonville, Fla.

1941-1942

OFFICERS

President—Eldon S. Dummit,
  Lexington, Ky.
Vice Presidents—
  Edwin E. Bibb, Norfolk, Va.
  William Rapp, Morton, Ill.
  R. Carter Tucker, Kansas City, Mo.
  G. K. Walters, Knoxville, Tenn.
Secretary-Treasurer—Russell F. Meyer,
  St. Louis, Mo.

EXECUTIVE COMMITTEE

Eldon S. Dummit; John N. Free, Immediate Past President, Wichita, Kan.; Thomas F. O'Keefe, Past President, Detroit, Mich.; R. Carter Tucker; Dr. Joseph J. Granata, Governor, Beaumont, Tex.; Ralph E. Hendee, Governor, Philadelphia, Pa.; Cyrus D. McCarron, Governor, Santa Monica, Calif.

1942-1943

OFFICERS

President—R. Carter Tucker,
Kansas City, Mo.
Vice Presidents—
Carl C. Donaugh, Portland, Ore.
W. D. Paul Farthing, Belleville, Ill.
Robert W. Newlon, Columbus, Ohio
Lucien L. Renuart, Miami, Fla.
Secretary-Treasurer—Russell F. Meyer,
St. Louis, Mo.

EXECUTIVE COMMITTEE

R. Carter Tucker; Eldon S. Dummit, Immediate Past President, Lexington, Ky.; John N. Free, Past President, Wichita, Kan.; Lucien L. Renuart; W. D. Paul Farthing; Dr. Joseph W. Seay, Governor, Trenton, N. J.; Lloyd M. Dalgleish, Governor, London, Ont.

1943-1944

OFFICERS

President—Theodore F. Peirce,
Los Angeles, Calif.
Vice Presidents—
Lloyd M. Dalgleish, London, Ont.
Julian S. Fleming, Louisville, Ky.
Bert E. Miller, Madison, Wis.
Dr. Joseph W. Seay,
Pennington, N. J.
Secretary-Treasurer—Russell F. Meyer,
St. Louis, Mo.

EXECUTIVE COMMITTEE

Theodore F. Peirce; R. Carter Tucker, Immediate Past President, Kansas City, Mo.; Eldon S. Dummit, Past President, Lexington, Ky.; Bert E. Miller; Dr. Joseph W. Seay; Emery Dennis, Governor, San Antonio, Tex.; Paul Wickham, Governor, Montreal, Que.

1944-1945

OFFICERS

President—Dr. Joseph W. Seay,
  Pennington, N.J.
Vice Presidents—
  Louis H. Grettenberger,
    Grand Rapids, Mich.
  A. S. Hull, Austin, Tex.
  Harry H. Loomis, Jeffersonville, Ind.
  J. Benton Webb, Washington, D. C.
Secretary-Treasurer—Russell F. Meyer,
  St. Louis, Mo.

EXECUTIVE COMMITTEE

Dr. Joseph W. Seay; Theodore F. Peirce, Immediate Past President, Los Angeles, Calif.; R. Carter Tucker, Past President, Kansas City, Mo.; A. S. Hull; J. Benton Webb; Raymond H. Fryberger, Governor, Minneapolis, Minn.; Willis S. Young, Governor, Lexington, Ky.

1945-1946

OFFICERS

President—Carl C. Donaugh,
  Portland, Ore.
Vice Presidents—
  Earle C. Dahlem,
    San Francisco, Calif.
  Raymond H. Fryberger,
    Minneapolis, Minn.
  Alvah S. Phillips, Wilmington, Del.
  William H. Pierce, Dallas, Tex.
Secretary-Treasurer—Russell F. Meyer,
  St. Louis, Mo.

EXECUTIVE COMMITTEE

Carl C. Donaugh; Dr. Joseph W. Seay, Immediate Past President, Pennington, N.J.; Theodore F. Peirce, Past President, Los Angeles, Calif.; Raymond H. Fryberger, Minneapolis, Minn.; William H. Pierce, Dallas, Tex.; Charles G. Klapheke, Governor, Louisville, Ky.; Frank L. Mallory, Governor, Windsor, Ont.

1946-1947
OFFICERS

President—William H. Pierce,
  Dallas, Tex.
Vice Presidents—
  Charles G. Klapheke, Louisville, Ky.
  Lucien L. Renuart, Miami, Fla.
  H. L. Scott, Corpus Christi, Tex.
  Charles W. Snyder, Detroit, Mich.
Secretary-Treasurer—Russell F. Meyer,
  St. Louis, Mo.

EXECUTIVE COMMITTEE

William H. Pierce; Carl C. Donaugh, Immediate Past President, Portland, Ore.; Dr. Joseph W. Seay, Past President, Pennington, N.J.; Charles G. Klapheke; Lucien L. Renuart; H. L. Scott; Charles W. Snyder; Guinn Huffsmith, Governor, Denver, Colo.; George A. Thomson, Governor, Memphis, Tenn.

1947-1948
OFFICERS

President—Lucien L. Renuart,
  Miami, Fla.
Vice Presidents—
  William W. Smythe, Welland, Ont.
  C. Milton Morris, Denver, Colo.
  Franklin A. Steinko,
    Washington, D. C.
  Cyrus D. McCarron,
    Santa Monica, Calif.
Secretary-Treasurer—Russell F. Meyer,
  St. Louis, Mo.

EXECUTIVE COMMITTEE

Lucien L. Renuart; William H. Pierce, Immediate Past President, Dallas, Tex.; Carl C. Donaugh, Past President, Portland, Ore.; C. Milton Morris; William W. Smythe; Franklin A. Steinko; Cyrus D. McCarron; Ed E. DeWees, Governor, San Antonio, Tex. W. A. Grant, Governor, London, Ont.

1948-1949

OFFICERS

President—C. Milton Morris,
Denver, Colo.
Vice Presidents—
Worth W. Caldwell, Portland, Ore.
J. Warren Day, Fort Worth, Tex.
Charles H. Sharrick, Lincoln, Neb.
Warren L. Stewart, Sharpsville, Pa.
Secretary-Treasurer—Russell F. Meyer,
St. Louis, Mo.

EXECUTIVE COMMITTEE

C. Milton Morris; Lucien L. Renuart, Immediate Past President, Miami, Fla.; William H. Pierce, Past President, Dallas, Tex.; Worth W. Caldwell; J. Warren Day; Charles H. Sharrick; Warren L. Stewart; George O. Browne, Governor, Indianapolis, Ind.; George J. Fella, Governor, Charlotte, N.C.

1949-1950

OFFICERS

President—Franklin A. Steinko,
Washington, D.C.
Vice Presidents—
George O. Browne, Indianapolis, Ind.
Frank L. Mallory, Windsor, Ont.
Dr. Elton C. Spires,
San Pedro, Calif.
George A. Thomson,
Memphis, Tenn.
Secretary-Treasurer—Russell F. Meyer,
St. Louis, Mo.

EXECUTIVE COMMITTEE

Franklin A. Steinko; C. Milton Morris, Immediate Past President, Denver, Colo.; Lucien L. Renuart, Past President, Miami, Fla.; George O. Browne; Frank L. Mallory; Dr. Elton C. Spires; George A. Thomson; Cornelius G. Coughlin, Governor, Erie, Pa.; Charles A. Shaw, Governor, Atlanta, Ga.

172

1950-1951

OFFICERS

President—George O. Browne,
  Indianapolis, Ind.
Vice Presidents—
  Lawrence J. Gibbons,
    Philadelphia, Pa.
  Roly P. Nall, Los Angeles, Calif.
  Ralph Stephenson, Moline, Ill.
  Ray S. Watt, El Paso, Tex.
Secretary-Treasurer—Russell F. Meyer,
  St. Louis, Mo.

EXECUTIVE COMMITTEE

George O. Browne; Franklin A. Steinko, Immediate Past President, Washington, D.C.; C. Milton Morris, Past President, Denver, Colo.; Lawrence J. Gibbons; Roly P. Nall; Ralph Stephenson; Ray S. Watt; Bernard G. Bell, Governor, Vancouver, Wash.; Jack Valero, Governor, Tampa, Fla.

1951-1952

OFFICERS

President—Roly P. Nall,
  Los Angeles, Calif.
Vice Presidents—
  Lawrence J. Gibbons,
    Philadelphia, Pa.
  Leo C. Lommel, Portland, Ore.
  Ralph Stephenson, Moline, Ill.
  Donald J. Twiss, M.D.,
    Brantford, Ont.
Secretary-Treasurer—Russell F. Meyer,
  St. Louis, Mo.

BOARD OF DIRECTORS

Roly P. Nall; George O. Browne, Immediate Past President, Indianapolis, Ind.; Franklin A. Steinko, Past President, Washington, D.C.; Lawrence J. Gibbons; Leo C. Lommel; Ralph Stephenson; Donald J. Twiss, M.D.; J. Warren Day, Fort Worth, Tex.; Joseph A. Peters, East St. Louis, Ill.; Jack Valero, Tampa, Fla.; Maurice M. Walsh, Birmingham, Ala.

1952-1953

OFFICERS

President—J. Warren Day,
Fort Worth, Tex.
Vice Presidents—
C. Lease Bussard, Frederick, Md.
Ralph E. Finney, Denver, Colo.
Maurice Perkins, Louisville, Ky.
Walter A. Reiling, M.D.,
Dayton, Ohio
Secretary-Treasurer—Russell F. Meyer,
St. Louis, Mo.

BOARD OF DIRECTORS

J. Warren Day; Roly P. Nall, Immediate Past President, Los Angeles, Calif.; George O. Browne, Past President, Indianapolis, Ind.; C. Lease Bussard; Ralph E. Finney; Maurice Perkins; Walter A. Reiling, M.D.; Ross D. Clarence, Toronto; Ont.; George W. Haycock, Arlington, N.J.; John S. Kelly, Kansas City, Kan.; Charles A. Shaw, Atlanta, Ga.

1953-1954

OFFICERS

President—Walter A. Reiling, M.D.,
Dayton, Ohio
Vice Presidents—
Lysle E. Fesler, Miami Beach, Fla.
Van W. Haverton, Peoria, Ill.
Harold M. Owen,
Battle Creek, Mich.
Edward J. Stolle, San Antonio, Tex.
Secretary-Treasurer—Russell F. Meyer,
St. Louis, Mo. (to Dec. 1953)
Secretary-Treasurer—Bernard B.
Burford, St. Louis, Mo. (Appointed
May 1954)

BOARD OF DIRECTORS

Walter A. Reiling, M.D.; J. Warren Day, Immediate Past President, Fort Worth, Tex.; Roly P. Nall, Past President, Los Angeles, Calif.; Lysle E. Fesler; Van W. Haverton; Harold M. Owen; Edward J. Stolle; Lloyd M. Dalgliesh, London, Ont.; Foster McCarl, Jr., Beaver Falls, Pa.; J. Harold Wilkins, Memphis, Tenn.; Gene D. Worl, Hagerstown, Ind.

174

1954-1955

OFFICERS

President—Maurice Perkins,
  Louisville, Ky.
Vice Presidents—
  Leslie M. Holtz, Glendale, Calif.
  Lee I. Ihle, Knoxville, Tenn.
  Nicholas C. Mueller, Baltimore, Md.
  William T. Tate, Dallas, Tex.
  Francis J. Nash, M.D.,
    Kansas City, Kan.
Secretary-Treasurer—Bernard B.
  Burford, St. Louis, Mo.

BOARD OF DIRECTORS

Maurice Perkins; Walter A. Reiling, M.D., Immediate Past President, Dayton, Ohio; J. Warren Day, Past President, Fort Worth, Tex.; Leslie M. Holtz; Lee I. Ihle; Nicholas C. Mueller; William T. Tate; Francis J. Nash, M.D.; Clark P. Oxley, San Francisco, Calif.; Melvin C. Reppen, Madison, Wis.; Donald J. Twiss, M.D., Brantford, Ont.

1955-1956

OFFICERS

President—Donald J. Twiss, M.D.,
  Brantford, Ont.
Vice Presidents—
  Charles T. Boyle, Richardson, Tex.
  R. A. Harp, Philadelphia, Pa.
  Francis J. Nash, M.D.,
    Kansas City, Kan.
  Richard F. Nazette,
    Cedar Rapids, Iowa
Secretary-Treasurer—Bernard B.
  Burford, St. Louis, Mo.

BOARD OF DIRECTORS

Donald J. Twiss, M.D.; Maurice Perkins, Immediate Past President, Louisville, Ky.; Walter A. Reiling, M.D., Past President, Dayton, Ohio; Charles T. Boyle; R. A. Harp; Francis J. Nash, M.D.; Richard F. Nazette; Ralph B. Bell, D.D.S., Washington, D.C.; Harold W. Copeland, Boulder, Colo.; Neil V. German, Calgary, Alta.; John W. Whatley, Atlanta, Ga.

1956-1957

OFFICERS

President—C. Lease Bussard,
Frederick, Md.
Vice Presidents—
Harold W. Brand, Houston, Tex.
Neil V. German, Calgary, Alta.
William E. Laswell, Evansville, Ind.
J. Harold Wilkins, Memphis, Tenn.
Secretary-Treasurer—Bernard B.
Burford, St. Louis, Mo.

BOARD OF DIRECTORS

C. Lease Bussard; Donald J. Twiss, M.D., Immediate Past President, Brantford, Ont.; Maurice Perkins, Past President, Louisville, Ky.; Harold W. Brand; Neil V. German; William E. Laswell, J. Harold Wilkins; Clarence J. April, Ann Arbor, Mich.; Charles E. Compton, Burbank, Calif.; Harry Naylor, Clearwater, Fla.; Edward A. Oppermann, Wichita, Kan.

1957-1958

OFFICERS

President—Harold W. Brand,
Houston, Tex.
Vice Presidents—
Jack O. Creasy, Columbia, Mo.
P. H. Frans, Holland, Mich.
S. Phil McCardwell, Louisville, Ky.
Phil D. McHugh,
Los Angeles, Calif.
Secretary-Treasurer—Bernard B.
Burford, St. Louis, Mo.

BOARD OF DIRECTORS

Harold W. Brand; C. Lease Bussard, Immediate Past President, Frederick, Md.; Donald J. Twiss, M.D., Past President, Brantford, Ont.; Jack O. Creasy; P. H. Frans; S. Phil McCardwell; Phil D. McHugh; E. Wendell Aske, Shelburne, Vt.; C. E. Gustafson, Austin, Tex.; John P. Harkins, Jackson, Miss.; Edwin P. Romanoski, Tucson, Ariz.

176

1958-1959

OFFICERS

President—J. Harold Wilkins,
 Memphis, Tenn.
Vice Presidents—
 Verlon Burrell, Dania, Fla.
 Lee E. Dodge, Sr., Denver, Colo.
 John M. Grimland, Jr.,
  Midland, Tex.
 Harold U. Mumma, Lancaster, Pa.
Secretary-Treasurer—Bernard B.
 Burford, St. Louis, Mo.

BOARD OF DIRECTORS

J. Harold Wilkins; Harold W. Brand, Immediate Past President,
Houston, Tex.; C. Lease Bussard, Past President, Frederick, Md.;
Verlon Burrell; Lee E. Dodge, Sr.; John M. Grimland, Jr.; Harold
U. Mumma; Hugh H. Cranford, Charlotte, N.C.; John W. Oakie,
Edmonton, Alta.; Raymond R. Rembolt, M.D., Iowa City, Iowa;
Walter H. Sebastian, Lexington, Ky.

1959-1960

OFFICERS

President—Nicholas C. Mueller,
 Baltimore, Md.
Vice Presidents—
 Ferguson Bell, Kansas City, Mo.
 George Cobley, M.D.,
  Santa Monica, Calif.
 John R. Olvey, Plainfield, Ind.
 Raymond R. Rembolt, M.D.,
  Iowa City, Iowa
Secretary-Treasurer—Bernard B.
 Burford, St. Louis, Mo.

BOARD OF DIRECTORS

Nicholas C. Mueller; Bernard B. Burford; J. Harold Wilkins,
Immediate Past President, Memphis, Tenn.; Harold W. Brand, Past
President, Houston, Tex.; Ferguson Bell; George Cobley, M.D.;
John R. Olvey; Raymond R. Rembolt, M.D.; John M. Aylen, Mon-
treal, Que.; Walter J. Baum, Sunnyvale, Calif.; Walter A. Heimsch,
Dayton, Ohio; William R. Smith, Sr., Shreveport, La.

177

1960-1961

OFFICERS

President—John W. Whatley,
   Atlanta, Ga.
Vice Presidents—
   Morris Cloninger, Beaumont, Tex.
   Walter H. Sebastian, Lexington, Ky.
   John M. Seidel, Columbus, Ohio
   Frank L. Smith, Jr., Lenoir, N.C.
Secretary-Treasurer—Bernard B.
   Burford, St. Louis, Mo.

BOARD OF DIRECTORS

John W. Whatley; Bernard B. Burford; Nicholas C. Mueller, Immediately Past President, Baltimore, Md.; J. Harold Wilkins, Past President, Memphis, Tenn.; Morris Cloninger; Walter H. Sebastian; John M. Seidel; Frank L. Smith, Jr.; Robert A. Brenholtz, Coatesville, Pa.; Irl C. Clary, D.D.S., Oswego, Ore.; Harold E. Loyns, Winnipeg, Man.; Alfred G. Waffle, Moline, Ill.

1961-1962

OFFICERS

President—Raymond R. Rembolt,
   M.D., Iowa City, Iowa
Vice Presidents—
   Frank Baker, Austin, Tex.
   W. Arnold Chambers,
      Chattanooga, Tenn.
   Gene H. Sternberg, Granite City, Ill.
   Ray L. Tillery, Denver, Colo.
Secretary-Treasurer—Bernard B.
   Burford, St. Louis, Mo.

BOARD OF DIRECTORS

Raymond R. Rembolt, M.D.; Bernard B. Burford; John W. Whatley, Immediate Past President, Atlanta, Ga.; Nicholas C. Mueller, Past President, Baltimore, Md.; Frank Baker; W. Arnold Chambers; Gene H. Sternberg; Ray L. Tillery; Hugh Crochetiere, Montreal, Que.; Foster McCarl, Sr., Fort Lauderdale, Fla.; Smith D. Miner, Ontario, Calif.; William R. Newhouse, Madison, Wis.

1962-1963

OFFICERS

President—John M. Grimland, Jr.,
  Midland, Tex.
Vice Presidents—
  Carl L. Bowen, D.D.S.,
    Albermarle, N.C.
  William R. Newhouse, Madison, Wis.
  Philip R. Reemes, Pine Bluff, Ark.
  Thomas A. Steele, Calgary, Alta.
Secretary-Treasurer—Bernard B.
  Burford, St. Louis, Mo.

BOARD OF DIRECTORS

John M. Grimland, Jr.; Bernard B. Burford; Raymond R. Rembolt, M.D., Immediate Past President, Iowa City, Iowa; John W. Whatley, Past President, Atlanta, Ga.; Carl L. Bowen, D.D.S.; William R. Newhouse; Philip R. Reemes; Thomas A. Steele; Levin H. Farmer, Jackson, Miss.; Robert H. Leonard, Knoxville, Tenn.; Thomas L. Roof, Tucson, Ariz.; Gordon S. Thompson, Evansville, Ind.

1963-1964

OFFICERS

President—George Cobley, M.D.,
  Santa Monica, Calif.
Vice Presidents—
  Levin H. Farmer, Jackson, Miss.
  Thomas L. Roof, Tucson, Ariz.
  James W. Tackett, Muskogee, Okla.
  Victor R. Zahn, Clifton, N.J.
Secretary-Treasurer—Bernard B.
  Burford, St. Louis, Mo.

BOARD OF DIRECTORS

George Cobley, M.D.; Bernard B. Burford; John M. Grimland, Jr., Immediate Past President, Midland, Tex.; Raymond R. Rembolt, M.D., Past President, Iowa City, Iowa; Levin H. Farmer; Thomas L. Roof; James W. Tackett; Victor R. Zahn; Dee L. Hopwood, Denver, Colo.; Alfred E. Percival, Ottawa, Ont.; S. Hunter Rentz, M.D., Columbia, S.C.; Robert W. Sloan, Manhattan, Kan.

1964-1965

OFFICERS

President—Carl L. Bowen, D.D.S.,
  Albemarle, N.C.
Vice Presidents—
  Dee L. Hopwood, Denver, Colo.
  Lysle Kindig, Kansas City, Mo.
  Robert H. Leonard, Knoxville, Tenn.
  A. Milton Radesky, Baltimore, Md.
Secretary-Treasurer—Bernard B.
  Burford, St. Louis, Mo.

BOARD OF DIRECTORS

Carl L. Bowen, D.D.S.; Bernard B. Burford; George Cobley, M.D.,
Immediate Past President, Santa Monica, Calif.; John M. Grim-
land, Jr., Past President, Midland, Tex.; Dee L. Hopwood; Lysle
Kindig; Robert H. Leonard; A. Milton Radesky; William S. Dick-
inson, Jr., Concord, Calif.; Jack W. Quick, Louisville, Ky.; Norman
L. Shipley, St. Catharines, Ont.; Raymond F. Wilhelm, O.D., Fort
Wayne, Ind.

1965-1966

OFFICERS

President—John R. Olvey,
  Plainfield, Ind.
Vice Presidents—
  Edwin L. Abbott, Ypsilanti, Mich.
  Robert M. Heidbrink,
   Minneapolis, Minn.
  Jack W. Quick, Louisville, Ky.
  Robert D. Rowe, Great Falls, Mont.
  Norman L. Shipley,
   St. Catharines, Ont.
  Robert W. Sloan, Manhattan, Kan.
  Thomas J. Terputac,
   Washington, Pa.
  Alfred A. Valdez,
   Albuquerque, N.M.
Executive Secretary—Bernard B.
  Burford, St. Louis, Mo.

BOARD OF DIRECTORS

John R. Olvey; Bernard B. Burford; Carl L. Bowen, D.D.S., Immedi-
ate Past President, Albemarle, N.C.; George Cobley, M.D., Past
President, Santa Monica, Calif.; Robert H. Leonard, President-Elect,
Knoxville, Tenn.; Edwin L. Abbott; Robert M. Heidbrink; Jack W.
Quick; Robert D. Rowe; Norman L. Shipley; Robert W. Sloan;
Thomas J. Terputac; Alfred A. Valdez

180

1966-1967

OFFICERS

President—Robert H. Leonard,
Knoxville, Tenn.
Vice Presidents—
Charles C. Campbell, Little Rock, Ark.
Dean F. Ferris, Youngstown, Ohio
Ralph Glasscock, Clinton, Mo.
Monroe Marlowe, Pasadena, Calif.
T. C. Parker, Houston, Tex.
Alfred E. Percival, Ottawa, Ont.
S. Hunter Rentz, M.D., Columbia, S. C.
Charles L. Temple, Denver, Colo.
Executive Secretary—Bernard B.
Burford, St. Louis, Mo. (Died—
July 13, 1966)
Hugh H. Cranford, St. Louis, Mo.
(Appointed Jan. 1, 1967)

BOARD OF DIRECTORS

Robert H. Leonard; Bernard B. Burford-Hugh H. Cranford; John R.
Olvey, Immediate Past President, Plainfield, Ind.; Carl L. Bowen,
D.D.S., Past President, Albemarle, N. C.; William R. Newhouse,
President-Elect, Madison, Wis.; Charles C. Campbell, Dean F.
Ferris; Ralph Glasscock; Monroe Marlowe; T. C. Parker; Alfred
E. Percival; S. Hunter Rentz, M.D.; Charles L. Temple.

1967-1968

OFFICERS

President—William R. Newhouse,
Madison, Wis.
Vice Presidents—
William E. Chitty, Norfolk, Va.
Phil E. Connell, Iowa City, Iowa
Walter G. Cook, Ft. Worth, Tex.
Daniel W. Ford, St. Petersburg, Fla.
Alford O. Leffler, Tempe, Ariz.
Richard S. McAnany, Shawnee, Kan.
Malcolm McDonald, Oakville, Ont.
Ronald E. Thompson, Tacoma, Wash.
Executive Secretary—Hugh H.
Cranford, St. Louis, Mo.

BOARD OF DIRECTORS

William R. Newhouse; Hugh H. Cranford; Robert H. Leonard,
Immediate Past President, Knoxville, Tenn.; John R. Olvey, Past
President, Plainfield, Ind.; Gene H. Sternberg, Sr., President-Elect,
Granite City, Ill.; William E. Chitty; Phil E. Connell; Walter G.
Cook; Daniel W. Ford; Alford O. Leffler; Richard S. McAnany;
Malcolm McDonald; Ronald E. Thompson.

1968-1969

OFFICERS

President—Gene H. Sternberg, Sr.,
  Granite City, Ill.
Vice Presidents—
  Roland E. Bradley, Gastonia, N. C.
  Mark H. Brooks, Oak Park, Ill.
  Hal B. Coleman, Clayton, Mo.
  Patrick L. Grady,
    Indianapolis, Ind.
  Harold E. Loyns, Winnipeg, Man.
  Dick R. Morrow, Denton, Tex.
  James B. Pretz, M.D.,
    Kansas City, Kan.
  Vincent H. Simpson,
    Pacific Palisades, Calif.
Executive Secretary—Hugh H.
  Cranford, St. Louis, Mo.

BOARD OF DIRECTORS

Gene H. Sternberg, Sr.; Hugh H. Cranford; William R. Newhouse, Immediate Past President, Madison, Wis.; Robert H. Leonard, Past President, Knoxville, Tenn.; Monroe Marlowe, President-Elect, Van Nuys, Calif.; Roland E. Bradley; Mark H. Brooks; Hal B. Coleman; Patrick L. Grady; Harold E. Loyns; Dick R. Morrow; James B. Pretz, M.D.; Vincent H. Simpson.

1969-1970

OFFICERS

President—Monroe Marlowe, Van Nuys, Calif.
Vice Presidents—
  Don L. Arnwine, Denver, Colo.
  Don W. Beal, Santa Rosa, Calif.
  Terrence M. Cassady,
    Burlington, Ont.
  Patrick L. Crooks, Wausau, Wis.
  Thomas M. Hill, San Antonio, Tex.
  Maurice F. Keathley, Jr.,
    Memphis, Tenn.
  Larrie H. Mason, M.D., Boise, Idaho
  W. B. Perry, Jr., East Point, Ga.
Executive Secretary—Hugh H.
  Cranford, St. Louis, Mo.

BOARD OF DIRECTORS

Monroe Marlowe; Hugh H. Cranford; Gene H. Sternberg, Sr., Immediate Past President, Granite City, Ill.; William R. Newhouse, Past President, Madison, Wis.; Charles C. Campbell, President-Elect, Little Rock, Ark.; Don L. Arnwine; Don W. Beal; Terrence M. Cassaday; Patrick L. Crooks; Thomas M. Hill; Maurice F. Keathley; Larrie H. Mason, M.D.; W. B. Perry, Jr.

182

1970-1971

OFFICERS
President—Charles C. Campbell,
Little Rock, Ark.
Vice Presidents—
Reginald R. Brown, Raleigh, N. C.
James E. Creed, D.V.M.,
Fort Collins, Colo.
Angelo P. Cupo, Clifton, N. J.
David J. Nolte, Madison, Wis.
Robert F. Nordhoff,
Baltimore, Md.
Benoit M. Parent, Ottawa, Ont.
Roger M. Shaw, Hialeah, Fla.
Dudley D. Williams,
San Diego, Calif.
Executive Secretary—Hugh H.
Cranford, St. Louis, Mo.

BOARD OF DIRECTORS
Charles C. Campbell; Hugh H. Cranford; Monroe Marlowe, Immediate Past President, Van Nuys, Calif.; Gene H. Sternberg, Sr., Past President, Granite City, Ill.; Norman L. Shipley, President-Elect, Union, Ont.; Reginald R. Brown; James E. Creed, D.V.M.; Angelo P. Cupo; David J. Nolte; Robert F. Nordhoff; Benoit M. Parent; Roger M. Shaw; Dudley D. Williams.

1971-1972

OFFICERS
President—Norman L. Shipley,
Union, Ont.
Vice Presidents—
Kenneth C. Emery,
San Antonio, Tex.
Otis T. Gray, Memphis, Tenn.
William H. Gum, Dayton, Ohio
Richard F. Price, Phoenix, Md.
M. Rudy Radofsky,
West Covina, Calif.
L. Alton Riggs, Jr., Mesa, Ariz.
Donald E. Strub, Iowa City, Iowa
Roger A. Teekell, Ph.D.,
Baton Rouge, La.
Executive Secretary—Hugh H.
Cranford, St. Louis, Mo.

BOARD OF DIRECTORS
Norman L. Shipley; Hugh H. Cranford; Charles C. Campbell, Immediate Past President, Little Rock, Ark.; Monroe Marlowe, Past President, Van Nuys, Calif.; S. Phil McCardwell, President-Elect, Louisville, Ky.; Kenneth C. Emery; Otis T. Gray; William H. Gum; Richard F. Price; M. Rudy Radofsky; L. Alton Riggs, Jr.; Donald E. Strub; Roger A. Teekell, Ph.D.

1972-1973

OFFICERS

President—S. Phil McCardwell,
Louisville, Ky.
Vice Presidents—
Phil Baker, Jr., Houston, Tex.
John W. Beanland, San Francisco, Calif.
Thomas H. Chapman, Red Deer, Alta.
Jack W. Fairall, El Paso, Tex.
Vernon D. Mitchell, Independence, Mo.
Seymour Silverman, Miami Beach, Fla.
Milton A. Snyder, Upper Darby, Pa.
J. Bryan Willingham, Jr., Atlanta, Ga.
Executive Secretary—Hugh H.
Cranford, St. Louis, Mo.

BOARD OF DIRECTORS

S. Phil McCardwell; Hugh H. Cranford; Norman L. Shipley, Immediate Past President, Union, Ont.; Charles C. Campbell, Past President, Little Rock, Ark.; Ronald E. Thompson, President-Elect, Tacoma, Wash.; Phil Baker, Jr.; John W. Beanland; Thomas H. Chapman; Jack W. Fairall; Vernon D. Mitchell; Seymour Silverman; Milton A. Snyder; J. Bryan Willingham, Jr.

1973-1974

OFFICERS

President—Ronald E. Thompson,
Tacoma, Wash.
Vice Presidents—
Lee O. Baker, Ph.D., Kalamazoo, Mich.
Benjamin L. Craig, Denver, Colo.
W. L. Johnson, Jacksonville, Fla.
Clarence L. Kennedy, Madison, Wis.
Peter J. Lombardi, Pasadena, Md.
William D. Mulinix, Midwest City, Okla.
Morton H. Nemy, Winnipeg, Man.
Bill J. Stewart, Kingsport, Tenn.
Executive Secretary—Hugh H.
Cranford, St. Louis, Mo.

BOARD OF DIRECTORS

Ronald E. Thompson; Hugh H. Cranford; S. Phil McCardwell, Immediate Past President, Louisville, Ky.; Norman L. Shipley, Past President, Port Stanley, Ont.; Ralph Glasscock, President-Elect, Clinton, Mo.; Lee O. Baker, Ph.D., Benjamin L. Craig; W. L. Johnson; Clarence L. Kennedy; Peter J. Lombardi; William D. Mulinix; Morton H. Nemy; Bill J. Stewart.

184

1974-1975

OFFICERS

President—Ralph Glasscock, Clinton, Mo.
Vice Presidents—
  Sam Bargamian, Tucson, Ariz.
  Pierre G. Bouchard, St. Laurent, Que.
  John B. Dodge, D.D.S., Tacoma, Wash.
  Donald J. Hand, San Antonio, Tex.
  David M. Hudson, Richmond, Va.
  Robert W. Lehman, Cedar Rapids, Ia.
  Art Long, Dayton, Ohio
  Robert H. Rogers, Jr., Shelby, N. C.
Executive Secretary—Hugh H.
  Cranford, St. Louis, Mo.

BOARD OF DIRECTORS

Ralph Glasscock; Hugh H. Cranford; Ronald E. Thompson, Imme-
diate Past President, Tacoma, Wash.; S. Phil McCardwell, Past Presi-
dent, Louisville, Ky.; Patrick L. Grady, President-Elect, Indianapolis,
Ind.; Sam Bargamian; Pierre G. Bouchard; John B. Dodge, D.D.S.;
Donald J. Hand; David M. Hudson; Robert W. Lehman; Art Long;
Robert H. Rogers, Jr.

1975-1976

OFFICERS

President—Patrick L. Grady,
  Indianapolis, Ind.
Vice Presidents—
  James E. Attarian, Sherman Oaks, Calif.
  Jesse M. Coker, Ed.D., Monticello, Ark.
  Arthur D. Derrough, St. Thomas, Ont.
  Truman M. Evans, Arlington, Tex.
  John B. Lawrence, Ardmore, Okla.
  Victor P. Reim, Jr., St. Paul, Minn.
  Richard L. Stoehr, Lincoln, Neb.
  James H. Yates, Phoenix, Md.
Executive Secretary—Hugh H.
  Cranford, St. Louis, Mo.

BOARD OF DIRECTORS

Patrick L. Grady; Hugh H. Cranford; Ralph Glasscock, Immediate
Past President, Clinton, Mo.; Ronald E. Thompson, Past President,
Tacoma, Wash.; Richard S. McAnany, President-Elect, Shawnee,
Kan.; James E. Attarian; Jesse M. Coker, Ed.D.; Arthur D. Derrough;
Truman M. Evans; John B. Lawrence; Victor P. Reim, Jr.; Richard
L. Stoehr; James H. Yates.

1976-1977

OFFICERS

President—Richard S. McAnany,
Shawnee, Kan.
Vice Presidents—
Paul Bilger, Jr., Lutherville, Md.
Harold J. Bond, Bossier City, La.
Lester R. Craft, Lake Waccamaw, N. C.
William L. Ewers, Tucson, Ariz.
Lionel Grenier, Terrebonne, Que.
Charles L. Hoberty, Indianapolis, Ind.
Gilbert L. Lorenz, St. Louis, Mo.
Roy V. Proctor, Salem, Ore.
Executive Secretary—Hugh H.
Cranford, St. Louis, Mo.

BOARD OF DIRECTORS

Richard S. McAnany; Hugh H. Cranford; Patrick L. Grady, Immediate Past President, Indianapolis, Ind.; Ralph Glasscock, Past President, Clinton, Mo.; Don L. Arnwine, President-Elect, Charleston, W. Va.; Paul Bilger, Jr.; Harold J. Bond; Lester R. Craft; William L. Ewers; Lionel Grenier; Charles L. Hoberty; Gilbert L. Lorenz; Roy V. Proctor.

1977-1978

OFFICERS

President—Don L. Arnwine,
Charleston, W. Va.
Vice Presidents—
A. Coy Dean, Alexander, Ark.
E. Noel Faddis, Pensacola, Fla.
Julian W. Johnson, Vienna, Va.
Kenneth E. Kile, Sr., Clinton, Tenn.
Merlan L. Marting, Dubuque, Ia.
Russell K. Osgood, Boulder, Colo.
William B. Scott, Jeffersonville, Ind.
Elmer Youck, Regina, Sask.
Executive Secretary—Hugh H.
Cranford, St. Louis, Mo.

BOARD OF DIRECTORS

Don L. Arnwine; Hugh H. Cranford; Richard S. McAnany, Immediate Past President, Shawnee, Kan.; Patrick L. Grady, Past President, Indianapolis, Ind.; Dudley D. Williams, President-Elect, LaJolla, Calif; A. Coy Dean; E. Noel Faddis; Julian W. Johnson; Kenneth E. Kile, Sr.; Merlan L. Marting; Russell K. Osgood; William B. Scott; Elmer Youck.

APPENDIX B
GROWTH OF OPTIMIST INTERNATIONAL

Year	Clubs	Membership	Year	Clubs	Membership
1919	11	1,298	1949	702	39,302
1920	15	1,770	1950	733	38,516
1921	26	3,068	1951	750	36,644
1922	49	4,000	1952	770	37,782
1923	59	4,500	1953	859	41,284
1924	88	5,566	1954	953	44,529
1925	112	7,142	1955	1,088	49,066
1926	130	8,215	1956	1,249	54,575
1927	140	8,584	1957	1,426	59,781
1928	177	8,454	1958	1,579	64,063
1929	119	7,254	1959	1,735	69,475
1930	122	7,000	1960	1,871	73,331
1931	125	6,000	1961	1,970	74,774
1932	123	7,399	1962	2,053	75,760
1933	110	4,600	1963	2,095	77,320
1934	106	5,200	1964	2,186	80,565
1935	112	6,121	1965	2,312	85,369
1936	128	7,016	1966	2,399	88,364
1937	149	8,582	1967	2,498	93,208
1938	172	9,498	1968	2,677	98,111
1939	198	10,381	1969	2,822	101,000
1940	234	12,175	1970	2,910	103,102
1941	259	13,260	1971	2,981	104,840
1942	264	12,895	1972	3,055	108,520
1943	251	12,391	1973	3,169	109,494
1944	247	14,081	1974	3,185	114,332
1945	251	16,049	1975	3,301	118,720
1946	331	23,016	1976	3,387	121,459
1947	467	31,181	1977	3,370	120,987
1948	592	36,610			

APPENDIX C

Conventions Of Optimist International

1—Louisville, Ky. 1919

2—St. Louis, Mo. 1920

3—Springfield, Ill. 1921

4—Kansas City, Mo. 1922

5—Chattanooga, Tenn. 1923

6—Milwaukee, Wis. 1924

7—Houston, Tex. 1925

8—Lexington, Ky. 1926

9—Denver, Colo. 1927

10—Asheville, N. C. 1928

11—Tulsa, Okla. 1929

12—Erie, Pa. 1930

13—Detroit, Mich. 1931

14—San Francisco, Calif. 1932

15—Washington, D. C. 1933

16—Toronto, Ont. 1934

17—St. Louis, Mo. 1935

18—Fort Worth, Tex. 1936

19—Cincinnati, Ohio 1937

20—Los Angeles, Calif. 1938

21—Richmond, Va. 1939

22—Kansas City, Mo. 1940

23—Minneapolis, Minn. 1941

24—Chicago, Ill.,
Wartime Conference 1942

25—Chicago, Ill.,
Wartime Conference 1943

26—St. Louis, Mo.,
Wartime Conference 1944

27—Minneapolis, Minn.,
Wartime Conference 1945

28—Miami Beach, Fla. 1946

29—Denver, Colo. 1947

30—San Antonio, Tex. 1948

31—San Francisco, Calif. 1949

32—Atlantic City, N. J. 1950

33—Detroit, Mich. 1951

34—Louisville, Ky. 1952

35—Washington, D. C. 1953

36—Houston, Tex. 1954

37—Montreal, Que. 1955

38—Los Angeles, Calif. 1956

39—Philadelphia, Pa. 1957

40—Dallas, Tex. 1958

41—Miami Beach, Fla. 1959

42—Grand Rapids, Mich. 1960

43—Las Vegas, Nev. 1961

44—St. Louis, Mo. 1962

45—Toronto, Ont. 1963

46—Denver, Colo. 1964

47—New Orleans, La. 1965

48—Baltimore, Md. 1966

49—Portland, Ore. 1967

50—Louisville, Ky. 1968

51—Miami Beach, Fla. 1969

52—Los Angeles, Calif. 1970

53—Minneapolis, Minn. 1971

54—Montreal, Que. 1972

55—San Antonio, Tex. 1973

56—Atlanta, Ga. 1974

57—San Francisco, Calif. 1975

58—Washington, D. C. 1976

59—Houston, Tex. 1977

60—San Diego, Calif. 1978

61—Kansas City, Mo. 1979

62—Toronto, Ont. 1980

63—Orlando, Fla. 1981

64—St. Louis, Mo. 1982